The Theater at Isthmia

The theater at Isthmia, looking north from the top of
the cavea.

The Theater at Isthmia

Elizabeth R. Gebhard

The University of Chicago Press
Chicago and London

International Standard Book Number: 0–226–28464–6
Library of Congress Catalog Card Number: 72–80813
The University of Chicago Press, Chicago 60637
The University of Chicago Press, Ltd., London

To my husband Paul

Contents

Illustrations

Illustrations

Abbreviations

AAG	Dinsmoor, W. *The Architecture of Ancient Greece*
AJA	*American Journal of Archaeology*
AM	*Mitteilungen des kaiserlich deutschen archäologischen Instituts: Athenische Abteilung*
Ant. Th.	Fiechter, E. *Antike griechische Theaterbauten*
BCH	*Bulletin de Correspondance Héllenique*
BSA	*Annual of the British School at Athens*
Daremberg-Saglio	*Dictionnaire des Antiquités Grecques et Romaines.* Edited by C. Daremberg and E. Saglio
Dörpfeld, *Gr. Th.*	Dörpfeld, W., and Reisch, E. *Das Griechische Theater*
IG	*Inscriptiones Graecae*
JIAN	*Journal International d'Archéologie Numismatique*
JOAI	*Jahreshefte des österreichischen archäologischen Instituts* in Wien
Papers ASCS	*Papers of the American School of Classical Studies in Athens*
RE	*Pauly's Realencyclopädie der klassischen Altertumswissenschaft*
von Gerkan, *Theater von Epidauros*	von Gerkan, A., and Müller-Wiener, W. *Das Theater von Epidauros*
Χαριστήριον	Χαριστήριον εἰς ᾿Αναστάσιον Κ. ᾿Ορλάνδον

Fig. 1. The theater looking north.

Preface

Ancient theaters were full of life. The most critical moments of man's existence were dramatized in tragedy, his most human side satirized in comedy, and songs to the flute and lyre hung on the clear air. The audience waved and shouted its approval or hooted unlucky actors out of the orchestra. Even now on the site of an ancient city where all other buildings lie buried, a few rows of broken seat blocks on a hillside frequently reveal the theater. There the visitor may recreate in his mind's eye the actors in the orchestra and imagine the animated spectators around him.

In the sanctuary of Poseidon on the Isthmus of Corinth the seat blocks from the theater are gone but the rim of the auditorium has always been visible above the ground. Although this theater, even after excavation, leaves much to be desired in terms of preservation, it is one of the earliest Greek theaters and it occupies an important place in the development of the theater as an architectural genre. Dramatic performances had not begun until the latter half of the sixth century B.C., and this meant that the theater as a structure also came relatively late to the Greek city scene. In the beginning a few wooden benches were put up to accommodate the spectators, and a temporary background structure may have been set up facing them. The memory of such an arrangement is found only in the late encyclopedias, and nothing of them has been identified in an excavation or could be expected to appear due to the perishable nature of the material. In the following years of the fifth century B.C. the basic elements of the theater were enlarged and elaborated to include some stone members, until by the second half of the fourth century some theaters were almost completely stone.

The Athenians appear to have been the first people, around the year 534 B.C., to include an embryonic tragedy in the series of dithyrambic choral songs presented in their annual festival to Dionysos. From the limited evidence available, this new art form seems to have involved the characterization of a figure from heroic mythology, who presented his problem in a speech or two. A chorus in turn responded to his situation and mourned his downfall. From these rudiments, or perhaps others with a slightly different emphasis, tragedy rapidly evolved with dialogue and action. Although some basic elements such as masks are attributed to Thespis, the traditional originator of the tragic idea, most innovations of the early years are grouped under the name of Aeschylus, the first of the great dramatic poets of the fifth century B.C., who was also producer and principal actor. As for the theater structure, one ancient report mentions the presence of wooden seats *(ikria)* in the agora, their collapse around 500 B.C., and their subsequent removal to the sanctuary of Dionysos on the south slope of the Akropolis.[1] Other lexicographers record a collapse

1. Photius, s.v. ἴκρια; cf. A. Pickard-Cambridge, *The Theatre of Dionysos in Athens*

of the *ikria* preliminary to the construction of an auditorium, without reference to the agora. This has led at least one modern scholar to believe that the performances were held in the sanctuary of Dionysos from the beginning, utilizing the front of the old temple to Dionysos as a background.[2] In any case, some particular place and arrangement for watching the dramatic contests was provided by the end of the sixth century B.C. By the final third of the fifth century supports for the wooden seats were made in stone and some stone foundations were introduced into the scene-building of the theater in the sanctuary of Dionysos, which by then was in the location that it would occupy with little change throughout the remainder of antiquity.

While drama seems to have made its first appearance in Athens, it quickly spread to other cities in Greece and to their colonies. Aeschylus traveled at least twice to Syracuse in Sicily, where he produced his plays between 472 and 467 B.C. and again after 458 B.C. A theater was provided by his host, and tradition supplies Damocopos as the name of the architect. At Corinth and elsewhere on the mainland and in Magna Graecia there was a local type of comic dance and mime performed by dancers in padded costumes who, by the fifth century B.C., may have played before a temporary scene-building with wooden seats for the spectators.[3] Later we hear of traveling groups of artists who performed at the major festivals,[4] carrying the works of Athenian poets to the cities of the Mediterranean world. Other offerings in their repertoire remain obscure. As interest in the drama spread, cities began to build permanent theater structures.

The ancient theater was actually composed of several distinct units and cannot accurately be called a building. The two major elements, auditorium (cavea) and scene-building (skene), were separated at each side by the entrance roads (parodoi), and the dancing floor (orchestra) lay between them. Perhaps the best example of a fully developed Greek theater complex is found at Epidauros. Pausanius singled it out as the most harmoniously proportioned of all Greek theaters, and since its excavation in the nineteenth century it has served as a model of the type in the minds of scholars and laymen alike. For many years all Greek theaters were reconstructed on the basis of this model, including the perfectly round orchestra

(Oxford: Clarendon Press, 1946), pp. 11–15, for other sources and a good discussion of the problem. See also G. Else, *The Origins and Early Form of Greek Tragedy* (Cambridge, Mass.: Harvard University Press, 1965).

2. T. B. L. Webster, "Staging and Scenery in the Ancient Greek Theatre," *Bulletin of the John Rylands Library* 42 (1960): 496–98.

3. Padded dancers appear on Corinthian vases from mid-seventh century to mid-sixth century B.C. and on two examples from the fourth century B.C.; see Webster, *Greek Theatre Production* (London: Methuen, 1956), pp. 99, 131–37.

4. Cf. A. Pickard-Cambridge, *The Dramatic Festivals of Athens*, rev. by J. Gould and D. Lewis (2d ed., rev.; Oxford: Clarendon Press, 1968), pp. 279 ff.

circle marked by a white marble curb that graphically unites the disparate forms of curved cavea and rectangular scene-building. After the excavation of other theaters, however, it became clear that all elements of a developed theater were not present in the earliest and simplest examples. The theater at Epidauros stands at the end of two centuries of theater building and represents perhaps the best solution to the design problems posed by the composite nature of the Greek theater.

Earlier and simpler theaters were designed on a less sophisticated plan, and in them we can best see the evolution of the architectural forms. Most scholars favor the orchestra as the original element of the theater where the chorus performed before drama, as such, was invented. In form, the orchestra has always been thought of as a circle. Indeed, the idea of a circular orchestra is so ingrained in all literature dealing with the theater, both structure and drama, that it will be worthwhile to examine briefly the origins of this idea and the reasons supporting it. Further discussion and specific references will be found in the footnotes to Chapter 1.

Before excavation of the Greek theaters themselves was undertaken, theories concerning the theater were derived from the description of a Greek theater in Vitruvius and from the Roman theaters that remained standing. To further complicate the picture, many Greek theaters had been remodeled on Roman lines during the imperial period. Thus little was known about the actual forms used earlier. The *kyklikoi choroi*, mentioned in literary sources in connection with the dithyramb, together with the basic circle for planning a theater as described by Vitruvius provided the first basis for the idea of a circular orchestra. Finally, when the theater at Epidauros was excavated, the complete and beautifully defined orchestra circle seemed to confirm this impression. There remained no doubt that the circle was the basic and original element of a Greek theater structure from the beginning.

When Wilhelm Dörpfeld began to uncover the early remains in the theater of Dionysos at Athens he was looking for evidence of the original orchestra circle. His conclusions appeared several years later in the first account of systematic investigations concerning the actual remains of Greek theaters, *Das Griechische Theater*, which he published with E. Reisch in 1896. At Athens, three small sections of polygonal masonry were found, one of which he assigned to the perimeter of the early orchestra and thus provided material evidence for the idea of a primary orchestra circle. His conclusions found immediate acceptance and are still repeated in many introductions to editions of the plays and in surveys of the ancient theater. For those concerned principally with the architectural problems of the theater, however, his orchestra presented a certain difficulty: no one could agree on the size of its diameter. A brief survey of the results of those who attempted to draw and measure it will show an elastic figure, stretching from 24 to 27 m. Dörpfeld originally gave the diameter as "around 24 m" in his text, and, after a question was raised on the basis of the size shown on his plan, he changed it to 27 m. J. T. Allen tried for greater precision with 26.84 m, Roy Flickinger reduced it to 25.26 m, C. Fensterbusch brought it back to 27.02 m, and W. Dinsmoor said 25.50 m. Finally, in 1935–36, E. Fiechter pointed out that Dörpfeld's segment of wall could not be part of a circle at all since its curve is irregular; it probably supported a ramp leading up to the orchestra terrace. But the orchestra circle remained. In spite of Fiechter's accurate description and removal of the one tangible piece of evidence for it, the existence of an orchestra circle was so ingrained in his thinking that he drew one on his revised plan even without material evidence, as Oscar Broneer pointed out in his review of the work. The circle had become an *idée fixe*, and so it continues to the present day.

Such a consideration of the orchestra circle may seem needlessly detailed, but the elastic diameter, the eventual removal of concrete evidence, and the continuation of the circle concept illustrate how pervasive the idea is, not only as a part of theater design, but as the first and basic element of the first theater. It is this conceptual certainty that has prevented a free consideration of other possible forms and an objective assessment of evidence for another form for the early Greek theater. When in 1947 C. Anti presented his theory suggesting a trapezoidal shape for the early orchestra it met with almost universal rejection. Although much of the difficulty came from his extension of sound conclusions reached at Syracuse to other theaters where no such evidence existed, the unqualified character of the rejection seems unwarranted. Critical ridicule has cast a pall over any thought of a rectilinear orchestra. After the discovery of a series of straight seat blocks and foundations for straight seats in the theater of Dionysos in Athens made it necessary to reconstruct a fifth-century cavea with straight seats, Dinsmoor in 1951 could not abandon the orchestra circle, but arranged the cavea as a nine-sided polygon around it. This is the most recent attempt to deal with the problem.

When we removed the lowest stratum of earth in the theater at Isthmia and discovered early water channels cut in clay (Pl. I), their converging arrangement again raised the question of the original shape of the Greek orchestra and cavea. The water channels were used merely to drain rainwater from the orchestra. Since they had a minimum importance in themselves, they would have been laid out to follow the lower edge of the cavea or a curb or walk delineating the area of the orchestra. All trace of the seats and orchestra from the first period at Isthmia has been cut away, but on the basis of the channels we can suggest with confidence that the cavea was three-sided, having a straight center section and wings diverging toward the skene. Other theaters also have been found wherein the seats are arranged in straight lines; the theater at Syracuse provides the closest parallel with a three-sided arrangement. In the theaters at Rhamnous, Ikaria, Tegea, and Morgantina, one or more straight rows are in place; at Athens the blocks remain but not *in situ*; at Argos and Thorikos straight and curved forms are combined. On the basis of the remains found in these theaters, the plan of the early or simple theater emerges as a series of straight seats for the spectators and a flat open space at the foot of the seats for the chorus and actors. The orchestra appears to have received no other definition than that provided by the seats and/or water channels where they occur. There is no indication of an orchestra circle or even curved seats.

In the concluding chapter (pp. 138-39) I have outlined a suggested sequence for the development of the theater, which begins with seats of honor at one side of an otherwise undefined area that was the dancing place or orchestra. Thus, instead of beginning with a predetermined form for the orchestra, the ancient architect first would have laid out the seating arrangement and then the scene-building opposite it, when there was one. The area between them, i.e., the orchestra, would have taken its shape from the line of the seats and the skene. Only in the more elaborate theaters built of stone in the later years of the fourth century B.C. was the orchestra delineated by a curb and conceived as a separate entity.

Turning now to the scene-building, we find that it too has been the subject of considerable debate, much of which has revolved around the existence of a raised stage and the time at which the proskenion was introduced. Perhaps more than the shape of the orchestra, the question of a stage affects our conceptions of how the plays were acted and produced. At first the elaborate scene-building and deep, low stage of the Roman theater were assumed for the Greek period also, but Dörpfeld showed that where these constructions existed in Greek theaters they were later additions. For the fifth and most of the fourth century B.C., he believed that all the major action took place in the orchestra and that the high colonnaded porch or proskenion was introduced at the same time as New Comedy. In recent years others have again suggested a low stage for the earliest period, but in connection with problems of production rather than as a result of new evidence from excavation.

On this problem the theater at Isthmia offers new material. Some kind of porch appears to have been constructed in front of the earliest wooden skene. Although the remains of this are slight, I have tried to show (pp. 17-21) that the proskenion was a necessary feature of any theater in which the orchestra was sunk below the natural ground level. The result of the sunken orchestra was that there was little or no first floor space inside the skene, and a proskenion provided the necessary "offstage" room for the performers. Therefore, the proskenion was not linked solely to the advent of New Comedy, as many have suggested, their basis being that the performances were then moved from the orchestra to the top of the pro-skenion. At Isthmia, the early proskenion not only gave "offstage" space to the performers in the orchestra but also provided a platform for contestants in the oratorical and musical events.

This raises another question concerning the ancient theater: what kind of performances were held there and how did the type of performance affect the basic shape and architectural detail of the theater? This is too broad a question for full exploration here, but several observations can be made on the basis of findings at Isthmia. First, the pertinacity of Greek forms during the Roman period is conspicuous. During two reconstructions, one in the first century A.D. and another in the second, the scene-building was almost completely rebuilt, each time reproducing the basic ground plan of the Greek skene, including the high, narrow proskenion. The cavea, too, in the reconstruction of the first century A.D., retained the diverging parodoi of its Greek predecessor. This conservatism in design is probably best explained by a certain continuity in the type of performances given there. The musical and oratorical contests for which the pro-skenion platform was most appropriate continued through the third century A.D. The absence of a barrier wall at the foot of the cavea shows that it was never adapted for animal fights or mock sea battles. Choral dances may have been performed in the orchestra, but the infringement on that space by two monumental columns in the second century makes it unlikely that after this time large-scale performances were held there.

Isthmia, then, was a place where the long Greek tradition of contests in music, oratory, acting, and drama survived the increasingly popular desire for more active sport. Persistence in program led to a continuity of design that was unusual for the ancient theater. It may have been just this continuation of traditional program that was responsible for the decline of interest in the festival toward the end of the third century. In other theaters, whether newly built or specially adapted for the purpose, acrobatics, animal shows, mimes, and aquatic spectaculars entertained spectators for at least another hundred years.

The uncovering of the Isthmia theater began as part of the University of Chicago excavations at the Isthmian Sanctuary of Poseidon, under the direction of Oscar Broneer. I commenced work there in the fall of 1959 as a student of Mr. Broneer and continued in the spring of 1960 and 1962 to complete the essential excavation of the theater. A study of the remains was presented as a doctoral dissertation in 1963 at the University of Chicago in the Department of Classical Languages and Literature under the supervision of Mr. Broneer and Robert L. Scranton. In the spring of 1967 I resumed excavation as a staff member of the University of California at Los Angeles excavations at Isthmia directed by Paul A. Clement. At present, with the exception of the cistern below the court, the entire theater has been uncovered.

Mr. Broneer provided the initial impetus and continuing encouragement for my work with Greek theaters, especially in connection with problems of the early orchestra and its rectilinear form. Throughout all phases of the work his help has been invaluable. On Mr. Broneer's retirement in 1960, Mr. Scranton assumed the official role of cosponsor for the dissertation, and he has generously given his time and good advice during the succeeding stages. Henry S. Robinson, Director of the American School of Classical Studies at Athens in the period 1959–69, deserves special appreciation for his valuable cooperation while I was in Greece and for his interest and later help at crucial points. For the 1967 season warm thanks go to Mr. Clement for providing the workmen necessary to complete excavation of the theater and the architect to draw new plans and revise earlier ones. G. Roger Edwards and John Hayes also merit particular gratitude for their patient examination of the anomalous pottery.

The plans and drawings are the result of the skill and kind cooperation of a number of architects: Alan Shapiro, John Travlos, Iro Athanasiades, the late Piet de Jong, Joseph W. Shaw, Richard Keating, and John G. Garner. It required outstanding care, eyesight, and patience to reproduce on paper the often vague cuttings in clay that are so much a part of the Isthmian theater.

The photographs included in this volume were taken by Mr. Broneer, with the exception of Figures 23, 31, 37, 48, 59, and 66, which are by Mr. Clement; the frontispiece and Figures 2, 4, 13, 14, 20, 32, 44, 49, 53, and 68 were taken by Mr. Seraf (PhotoEmile).

Finally, my greatest appreciation goes to Paul G. Gebhard and Luther I. Replogle for their constant and unlimited support throughout all the years of this work.

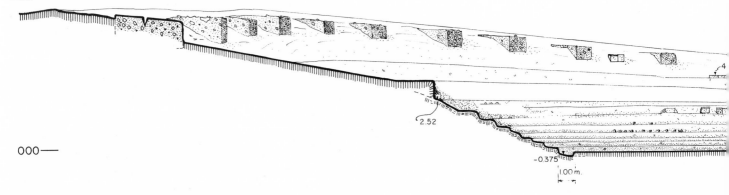

Pl. II. Section through the north-south axis, looking west.

Introduction

The theater at Isthmia is located on a slope about 80 m northeast of the Temple of Poseidon, on one side of the rocky plateau that gave the temple such a commanding view from the Corinthian to the Saronic gulfs. The auditorium faces north toward the neck of the isthmus, which is still covered with the pine trees characteristic of the place in ancient times (frontispiece, Fig. 1).[1] Although the slope is not very steep, it was the only one suitable for a theater, and the depression left by an old stream bed would have facilitated the task of constructing the cavea. The north-south axis corresponds approximately to the stream bed, which includes the area beneath section III of the scene-building (Pl. I).[2]

The natural hillside would have allowed only a few of the spectators a good view of the performances, with the consequence that some method of steepening the incline was needed. In other theaters with a similar problem the remedy was either to add earth at the top of the slope with the necessary retaining walls or to dig out a hollow at the foot of the hill. For a small theater, as at Isthmia, the latter method would have been easier and was the one chosen. The foundations for several rows of seats were then cut into the sides of the artificial hollow (Pl. II). The bottom of the hollow was leveled for the orchestra floor, thereby creating the effect of a

1. Pausanius, *Τῆς Ἑλλάδος Περιήγησις*, ii. 1. 7. See Pl. IX, p. 92, for site plan of ancient Isthmia.
2. The theater is actually oriented slightly north by northeast (Pl. II), but for the purposes of this discussion the axis will be considered to run due north and south.

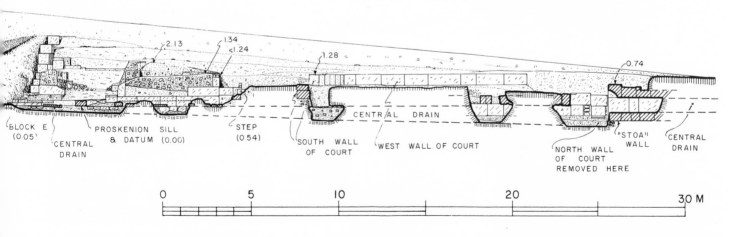

JOSEPH W. SHAW
1965, 1970

sunken orchestra or one that lies below the natural level of the hill (Figs. 1, 2). An analogous arrangement is found in the theaters at Eretria, Sikyon, Oropos, and Corinth. The fact that these theaters have certain features in common will be helpful in reconstructing the theater at Isthmia.

The hollowing-out process left a vertical scarp 1 to 2 m high at the north edge of the orchestra on which the scene-building was constructed with only a central passageway open at orchestra level. Entrance roads or parodoi cut from the hill led down into the orchestra at both sides. Behind the scene-building or skene (the terms are used interchangeably throughout the text) the slope originally continued its descent to the north and east, although in Roman times the area was made level with the addition of artificial fill.

Fig. 2. The artificial hollow of the cavea and foundation cuttings for seats, looking west; concrete foundations for piers in the background.

At the southeast edge of the cavea, under the series of concrete foundations for the cavea from the Roman period, an outcropping of bedrock appears at the fifth foundation from the east end and forms a ledge stretching toward the southwest (Pl. I). Beneath the ledge a large cave with two main chambers and two courtyards was carved out of the clay.[3] The clay-cut couches inside the chambers and the kitchen facilities in the courtyards give ample indication that the cave was used for dining purposes. In the northeast corner of the western courtyard a small storage pit lined with fine stucco contained seventeen kitchen pots carefully stacked upside down where their last user had stored them away before the cave was abandoned in the middle of the fourth century B.C.[4] The cave chambers were opened again in the second century A.D. during the laying of the foundations for the cavea, and they may have been used for storage and later as a dumping ground, judging from the debris found inside. The close proximity and contemporaneity between the cave and the theater makes it likely that there was some connection between them; perhaps the cave served as headquarters for the performers' guild known as the Artists of Dionysos (οἱ περὶ τὸν Διόνυσον τεχνῖται), which was active at Isthmia.[5] Officials called "Guardians of the Grotto" are mentioned in a mid-second-century A.D. inscription from Italy in connection with a cult society of Dionysos.[6]

The theater and later stadium were the two monuments of the Isthmian sanctuary that were readily recognizable before the Temple of Poseidon was finally located and identified in 1952.[7] E. Curtius and C. Bursian mention the theater as being outside the so-called Fortress of Justinian, which they identified as the precinct of Poseidon, and the theater is marked on Bursian's Plate I, 1.[8] The semicircle of concrete foundations for the

---

3. A full account of the cave appears in O. Broneer, *Isthmia II, Topography and Architecture*, American School of Classical Studies at Athens (in press); see also Broneer, "Isthmia: Campaign of 1959," *Archaeology* 13 (1960): 109; Broneer, "Excavations at Isthmia, 1959–1961," *Hesperia* 31 (1962): 4–7, Fig. 3.

4. Ibid., p. 6, Pl. 12a-f.

5. A chapter on the Artists of Dionysos is included in A. Pickard-Cambridge, *The Dramatic Festivals of Athens* (2d ed., rev.; Oxford: Clarendon Press, 1968), pp. 279 ff. The guild at Isthmia appears in an inscription from Thespiai of 250 B.C. (ibid., pp. 292–93), and in one from Argos (*IG* 4: 558). The guild at Syracuse is discussed by G. Rizzo, *Il Teatro Greco di Siracusa* (Milan: Bestetti and Tumminelli, 1923), pp. 123–33, in connection with a rock-hewn grotto at the top of the cavea. See M. Bieber, *The History of the Greek and Roman Theater* (2d ed., rev.; Princeton: Princeton University Press, 1961), pp. 84–85, n. 30. None of the ancient references, however, can be dated as early as the Isthmian cave.

6. The whole question is thoroughly discussed by A. Vogliano and F. Cumont, "La grande Iscrizione Bacchica del Metropolitan Museum," *AJA* 37 (1933): 215–26, 258–60.

7. O. Broneer, "Isthmia Excavations, 1952," *Hesperia* 22 (1953): 185–89.

8. E. Curtius, *Peloponnesos* (2 vols.; Gotha: Justus Perthes, 1851–52), 2: 542; C. Bursian, *Geographie von Griechenland* (2 vols.; Leipzig: B. G. Teubner, 1862–72), 2: 21, Pl. I, 1. Recently discovered evidence seems to indicate a date earlier than the time of Justinian for the fortress, P. Clement, "Isthmia," Ἀρχαιολογικὸν Δελτίον 23 (1968): 140.

cavea, which was the only part of the structure visible at that time, naturally gave rise to the opinion that it was a Roman theater. P. Monceaux believed that he had located a Greek theater nearby, but there are no remains now that could support that identification.[9] Good summaries of the information available about the theater before its excavation are given in *RE* and Daremberg-Saglio under "Isthmia"; they also include a catalogue of the ancient sources regarding contests in the theater.[10] J. Jenkins and H. Megaw mention the theater in connection with their investigation of the Isthmia, but they did not explore it.[11]

The first trench in the theater (70 m long by 4 m wide) was dug during the 1954 season of the University of Chicago's Isthmian excavation (Fig. 3).[12] It revealed a section of the seat cuttings, proskenion sill, skene, and court, but the poor state of preservation discouraged further work at that time. In 1957 more clearing was done in the west end of the west parodos where the discovery of a marble head representing a youth wearing the pine crown of an Isthmian victor (IS 351) aroused fresh interest in the building.[13] The systematic excavation of the whole theater was then carried out during the fall of 1959 and the spring seasons of 1960, 1962, and 1967 under the direction of Oscar Broneer and the author.[14]

The material remains of the theater are not extensive, but they are sufficient to permit identification of the several reconstructions of the building and the basic plan in each case. The rim of the cavea is outlined by a semicircle of concrete foundations, which has an outside diameter of about 72 m. Farther down the slope a series of steplike foundation cuttings in the hard clay of the hill supported the lower rows of seats. The foundations now visible are from the third and last reconstruction of the cavea, which obliterated the cuttings from two earlier arrangements. A circular manhole in the orchestra (labeled 1 on Pl. I) led to an underground drain belonging to the first Greek period, and a clay-cut channel conducted water to the manhole. The pair of square foundations that occupy such a prominent place in the orchestra supported two ornamental Ionic columns that have been recovered from the so-called Fortress of Justinian. Along

9. P. Monceaux, "Fouilles et Recherches Archéologiques au Sanctuaire des Jeux Isthmiques," *Gazette Archéologique* 10 (1885): 208 ff.

10. K. Schneider, "Isthmia," *RE* 18 (1916): 2248 ff.; L. Couve, "Isthmia," Daremberg-Saglio, 3, Part 1 (1899): 588 ff.

11. J. Jenkins and H. Megaw, "Researches at Isthmia," *BSA* 32 (1931–32): 68 ff., Pl. 26.

12. O. Broneer, "Excavations at Isthmia, 1954," *Hesperia* 24 (1955): 122–23, Pls. 41a, 48a-b.

13. O. Broneer, "Excavations at Isthmia, Fourth Campaign, 1957–1958," *Hesperia* 28 (1959): 319 f., 326, no. 3, Pls. 64a, 66a; O. Broneer, "The Isthmian Victory Crown," *AJA* 66 (1962): 259–63.

14. Preliminary reports on the theater have been published by Broneer in *Archaeology* 13 (1960): 105–9; *Hesperia* 31 (1962): 7–10, Fig. 4; "Isthmiaca," *Klio* 39 (1961): 264–68.

Fig. 3. The first trench dug in the theater, 1954;
orchestra and cavea, looking south.

the north side of the orchestra the proskenion sill is in place, and behind
it was a retaining wall for the scarp, of which only the first course on the
west side remains. Beneath the scene-building a passageway through the
bank connected the orchestra with the area behind the scene-building.
The foundations for the building date from Roman times and reveal that
it was then divided into four rooms (sections I, II, III–IV, V on Pl I)[15] or
possibly five if the east wing was divided into two rooms as was the case on
the west side. All vestiges of earlier buildings at this level have disappeared.
In the west parodos, walls that supported a concrete vault are partially preserved; on the east side only foundations or in some places beddings are
left from similar walls. The lower courses of ashlar retaining walls for the

15. The rectangular concrete foundations of the second scene-building on Pl. I have been
numbered I to V for reference. Although they are called room I, etc., in the text, it should
be remembered that "rooms" III and IV very likely represent a single room above the level
of the foundations.

cavea remain from the first Roman period; the western one stands to a height of one or two courses for its entire length.

The area behind the scene-building was enclosed by four walls, the foundations of which are best preserved on the south and west sides. There seems to have been a large, irregularly shaped court that was devoid of any permanent interior construction (Fig. 4). Entrance to the theater from the north was provided by two roads along the east and west sides of the court, leading into the parodoi. Beyond the road on the west side the slope was divided into two terraces by walls c-c and e-e (Pl. I). On the east side our excavations included only a narrow portion beyond the road where a storeroom occupied the south end and the first and second northeast buildings succeeded each other at the north.[16]

A drain under the floor of the central passage beneath the skene carried off water from the orchestra after the earlier drainage system fed by manhole 1 was abandoned. Another drain entering the theater from the southeast joined the central drain near the north wall of the court.

Earlier material on the site includes some prehistoric sherds found at the bottom of the old stream bed immediately above virgin clay inside section III of the skene. They were probably washed down from farther up the slope. The deposit was principally Early Helladic but included also a few Mycenaean sherds.[17]

In addition to the pottery and at a higher level are three short stretches of a rough polygonal wall that were incorporated into the concrete foundations of the skene (III, IV on Pl. I). The largest segment, which runs northeast-southwest, lies in the north wall of section IV. Another piece in line with the first was built into the east wall of section III (Fig. 5). The westernmost stretch lies north of section III and runs northwest-southeast. All the segments are constructed with uncut stones of varying sizes, laid without mortar and with the uneven face toward the outside or northwest and northeast respectively. The easternmost wall (in section IV) rests on the native clay of the bank; the segment west of it is at the same level but bedded on the silt that filled the old stream bed. The westernmost portion rests on hardpan at a slightly lower level. The three stretches of wall appear to have belonged to two sides of the same structure, and they would have met to form a corner greater than ninety degrees. No sherds that could be used to determine their date were found nearby, but their orientation obviates any connection with the theater. Furthermore, they must post date the stream that flowed down the hill in prehistoric times because they rest partially on the silt that filled its bed.

---

16. The walls of the first northeast building are shown in outline on Pl. I.
17. See E. Smith, "Prehistoric Pottery from the Isthmia," *Hesperia* 24 (1955): 142.

Fig. 4. The scene-building and court, looking northwest from the top of the east parodos.

Fig. 5. The west half of the cavea from the scene-building, looking southwest. Segment of polygonal wall marked (a).

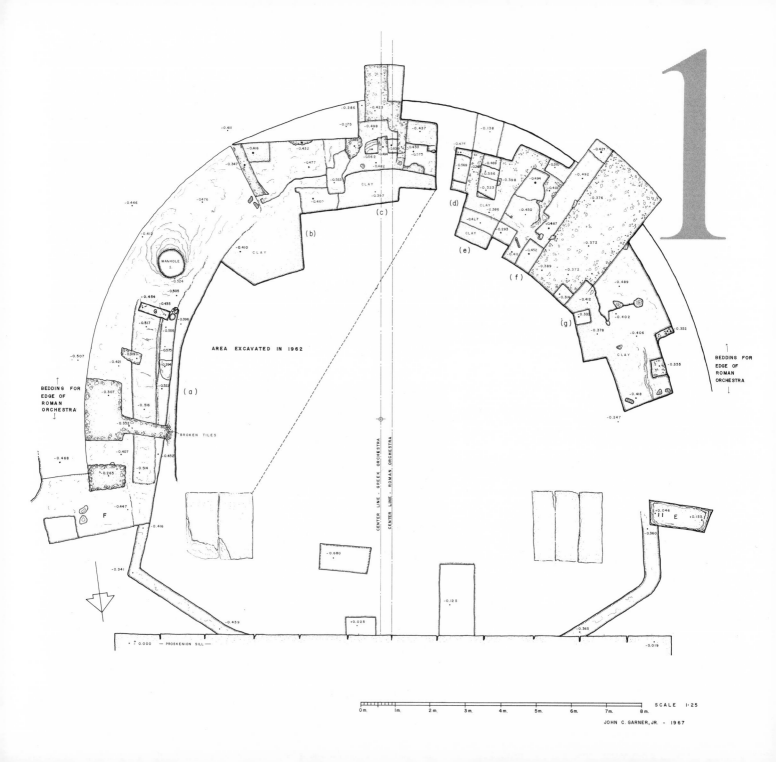

MANHOLE 1

AREA EXCAVATED IN 1962

BEDDING FOR
EDGE OF
ROMAN
ORCHESTRA

BEDDING FOR
EDGE OF
ROMAN
ORCHESTRA

CLAY

CLAY

CLAY

CLAY

CLAY

CLAY

BROKEN TILES

CENTER LINE - GREEK ORCHESTRA

CENTER LINE - ROMAN ORCHESTRA

G

F

E

(a)

(b)

(c)

(d)

(e)

(f)

(g)

• 0.000 — PROSKENION SILL —

SCALE 1·25

0 m.   1 m.   2 m.   3 m.   4 m.   5 m.   6 m.   7 m.   8 m.

JOHN C. GARNER, JR. - 1967

1

The First Greek Period

The Orchestra and Cavea

The hollow that accommodates the cavea and orchestra was cut from hard, rocklike clay[1] that also includes veins of soft, sandy material, especially on the west side. The uneven surface at the bottom of the hollow was probably covered by a layer of earth and clay packed hard to make the orchestra floor, although none of the ancient floor remains.[2] The clay surface that is now preserved slopes gently toward the south except for the area surrounding manhole 1 where the slope is more pronounced.[3]

As it appears today, two narrow channels cut in clay constitute the principal feature of the early orchestra. They were intended for drainage purposes and would have lain at the edge of the orchestra. The channel on the east side is the best preserved (Pls. I, III, Figs. 6, 7). It begins near the west end of block G in the orchestra and is 0.40 m wide and about 0.15 m deep at present, with the bottom at a level of −0.55 m. From block G the first segment of the channel runs almost due north in a straight line[4] for 7.55 m to cutting F. Beginning at a point 1.60 m north of block G, the east side of the channel was encroached upon in the succeeding period by the bedding for the paved walk at the foot of the cavea (Fig. 6, chap. 2, p. 35), but the west side is well preserved. In the section north of cutting F the channel, with both sides intact, narrows to 0.30 m. It then makes a 110° turn to the northwest, and at the south edge of the proskenion sill it makes another slight turn to the west just before being blocked by the sill. The final section north of the sill running almost due west ends at the edge of the later central drain.

The northern sections of the channel have their counterpart on the west side of the orchestra where a similar channel begins near block E[5] (Pls. I, III, Fig. 8). Due to the soft, sandy consistency of the bedrock in this area, the sides have crumbled slightly, though the outline is clear. The channel is 0.45 m wide and now 0.20 m deep, and it makes the same strong bend as on the east side. Although the two channels vary slightly in detail, they are comparable in design and belong to the same plan.

The function of the channels seems to have been to lead off rainwater that collected in the orchestra. Drainage was a problem in any theater

1. This kind of clay is technically known as marl, and it is very common around the isthmus.
2. Sherds from the third and fourth centuries A.D. were found in the fill immediately above hardpan (chap. 4, pp. 134–35).
3. The entire grade drops only 0.40 m from the proskenion to the south side of the orchestra. The zero point for all levels in the theater is located at the east end of the proskenion sill, 39.83 m above sea level and 13.54 m below the Temple of Poseidon datum point.
4. The irregularity seems to be the result of carelessness in cutting the channel, which was intended to be straight.
5. The fact that the channel does not now continue as far south as the one on the east may be the result of later alterations in the orchestra.

Pl. III. The Greek orchestra.

Fig. 6. The east channel in the first Greek orchestra, looking north from manhole 1. Block G in the foreground. West edge of channel marked by shadow. Bedding for walk at east edge of second Greek orchestra at right.

because the cavea formed a great funnel directing the water down into the orchestra. A sunken orchestra further compounded the problem by being the lowest point in the area and by lowering the departure point of the drainage system that then required a long stretch of underground drain to carry off the water. The northern portions of both channels slope toward the north; the eastern one drops 0.14 m from the bend to the mouth, and a similar slope was probably intended on the west. Furthermore, both channels end within a short distance of each other at the north. The intention seems to have been a drain under the central passage (in the same place as the later central drain) to receive the flow from the side channels, but there are indications that this plan never was put into effect. Significant in this respect is the absence of dark silt in the bottom of the channels that would have accumulated during use and the fact that at the time of excavation they were filled with hard-packed chunks of clay as if they had been blocked up soon after they were dug. This was especially apparent on the east side. In addition, it is unlikely that a completed central drain would have been immediately replaced by another extensive underground drain that began at manhole 1 and was clearly in use during the first period. Consequently, the plan for draining the orchestra seems to have been changed after the channels were dug, and the water was led not toward the central passage but into manhole 1. For this purpose the bottom of the eastern drain south of the bend was recut so that it sloped in the direction of the

Fig. 7. The east channel (on the left), looking southeast with the proskenion sill in foreground.

Fig. 8. West channel in first Greek orchestra, looking south.

manhole, with a total drop of 0.22 m. The undisturbed portions of this channel south of the bend were indeed filled with a dark silt at the time of excavation, attesting to a considerable period of use. Similar channels along the west and south sides of the orchestra may also have emptied into manhole 1, but later disturbances in the orchestra have obliterated them. The sandy nature of the bedrock on the west and southwest sides is particularly unsuited to preserving the form of any cuttings made in it.

The large drainage system entered by manhole 1 was an extensive undertaking and a rather surprising one in view of the relatively simple character of the early theater as it appears to us. It simply confirms the importance of orchestra drainage in an outdoor theater, especially in one with a sunken orchestra.

The circular shaft of manhole 1 (0.78 m in diameter) is 2.18 m deep and is furnished with two sets of foot holes cut into the sides.[6] At the bottom the long drain begins, 0.94 m high and 0.55 m wide, hollowed out of virgin clay and cut with an arched roof. A second manhole (2, Pl. I) gave access to the drain 23.50 m north of manhole 1; it is oval, 0.93 m by 0.59 m. The south wall of the court later extended over the north edge of the manhole, which by that time was filled with earth, stones, and broken pottery.[7] A stone that seems to have been the original cover-slab was found lying on edge inside the manhole. It measures 0.75 m in preserved length (one end is broken off) and is 0.11 m thick. The third manhole (3, Pl. I), 19.75 m farther north, was blocked by the rear (north) wall of the court and was filled with mortar and stones.[8] The height of the drain decreases as it continues northward, and the width increases to 0.90 m; the floor descends markedly. At a distance of 8.65 m from manhole 3 the drain meets an east-west channel (at no. 4 on Pl. I), the floor of which is about 2.25 m below

6. See Broneer, *Hesperia* 31 (1962): 7, for a preliminary mention of the underground drain. The manholes are numbered 1, 2, 3, 5 on Pl. I. Point 4 on Pl. I indicates a clearing made over an opening in the roof of the drain that was not an original manhole. A manhole in the orchestra connected to an underground drain also is found in the theaters at Segesta and Sikyon, where both the manhole and drain passage were used by actors as well.

7. All the manholes of the drain were filled with stones, anomalous pieces of conglomerate, and firmly packed earth that contained pieces of coarse vessels and some finer ware described below, pp. 24–26. The manhole in the orchestra appears to have been disturbed in Roman times because a few possibly later sherds were found in the predominantly Greek fill. The other manholes were also opened later, once apparently in the first century A.D. and again in the second century in connection with the construction of the court. The shaft deposits were stratified, however, with undisturbed Greek material at the bottom.

8. The actual manhole may have lain a little farther north, but at this point the foundations for the double north wall of the court and stoa interrupted the drain and an opening had to be made from the top in order to continue excavation of the channel. Another drain, 1.10 m wide, may have entered the main theater drain from the west along the line of the later court wall; or it is possible that the wall had an exceptionally deep foundation trench. In any case, the opening is completely filled with Roman masonry, making further excavation impossible.

the floor of the theater drain. The intersection must have been planned when the theater drain was constructed because the floor starts to descend about 3.80 m before it meets the older east-west channel. The east-west drain is also rock-cut, but it is not as straight or as regularly finished as the theater drain. At the bottom is a stuccoed conduit, 0.20 m wide at the top and 0.14 m deep but with considerable variation in both dimensions. It seems that this was originally intended to carry fresh water since it is carefully stuccoed, but later it must have served as a drain, at least by the time of the theater drain that emptied into it. The western extension of the east-west channel beyond point no. 4 is filled with the rubble masonry of a Roman foundation[9] that coincides with the channel for the small section that was uncovered; the eastern section was cleared for 12.10 m from the junction with the theater drain at point no. 4 to point no. 5 (Pl. I). Here, another oval manhole opened into the drain, but it was not cleared and the excavation was carried no further.

One more feature remains that may be assigned to the orchestra of this period. It is a rectangular cutting, 1.35 m long, 0.66 m wide, and 0.35 to 0.40 m deep, (Pls. I, III), located 1.85 m south of the proskenion and slightly to the east of the central axis. Its depth and shape suggest that it was cut to receive a foundation block or blocks, perhaps to support an altar.[10] Its orientation with the slanted course of the eastern drainage channel rather than with the line of the proskenion associates it with the first period. Sherds from the first century A.D. found in the bottom indicate that the foundation was removed at the time of the first Roman remodeling.

9. See chap. 4, pp. 116–17, for a description of this wall that seems to have been intended as the front wall of a "stoa," later left incomplete. Only the rubble foundation placed over the drain could be shown on the plan (Pl. I).

10. Although it has long been inferred from literary sources (e.g., Pollux, *Onomasticon* iv. 101, 123) that an altar regularly occupied the center of the orchestra (W. Dörpfeld and E. Reisch, *Das Griechische Theater*, [Athens: Barth and von Hirst, 1896], pp. 33–36; W. Dinsmoor, *The Architecture of Ancient Greece* [London: B. T. Batsford, 1950], p. 314; M. Bieber, *The History of the Greek and Roman Theater* [2d ed., rev.; Princeton: Princeton University Press, 1961], pp. 55 ff.), E. Bethe pointed out long ago that no altar had been found *in situ* in the orchestra, and there is very little evidence that the choros danced around an altar in the center of the orchestra ("Der Spielplatz des Aischylos," *Hermes* 59 [1924]: 112 f.), and he was later supported by Roy Flickinger ("The Theater of Aeschylus," *TAPA* 61 [1930]: 94–95). The same point has been recently affirmed by A. von Gerkan and W. Müller-Wiener (*Das Theater von Epidauros* [Stuttgart: W. Kohlhammer, 1961], p. 8, n. 6). At Thorikos, however, a rectangular foundation set into a recess in the cavea at one side of the orchestra very likely supported an altar as part of the original plan; or it may date from the time of its remodeling (cf. C. Anti, *Teatri Greci Arcaici* [Padua: Le Tre Venezie, 1947], pp. 48, 145, Fig. 13; P. Arias, *Il Teatro greco fuori di Atene* [Florence: G. S. Sansoni, 1934], pp. 26–28; O. Dilke, "Details and Chronology of Greek Theatre Caveas," *BSA* 45 [1950]: 26). T. Hackins in his recent exploration and study of the remains at Thorikos states that the altar appears to be contemporary with the construction of the stone seats, which he places toward the middle of the fifth century B.C. ("Le Théâtre," *Thorikos 1965* 3 [1967]: 93–95, Fig. 139).

The edge of the early orchestra on the east, west, and probably south sides was very likely defined by the open drainage channels south of the bend.[11] On the north side the front of the skene would have closed the orchestra area.

The problem of which was planned first, the form that the cavea was to take or the shape of the orchestra, is similar to the one involving the chicken and the egg, and the absence of contemporary records precludes a final answer. Yet, from a practical point of view and in terms of construction of the Isthmian theater, some suggestions may be made. The inadequate slope of the hill most convenient to the temple necessitated the large-scale excavation of a hollow to accommodate the cavea and orchestra. This operation undoubtedly involved the greatest amount of work and expense, and the decisions related to it, such as size and intended seating capacity, would have been the first to be made while the theater was in the planning stage. And with these considerations naturally would have gone the question of what form the cavea was to take. Decisions regarding the other elements, such as placement of scene-building and drainage, would have followed those concerning the cavea in the planning stage as they almost certainly did in construction. With a sequence as outlined above it would follow that the form of the orchestra was determined by the form decided upon for the cavea.[12]

11. In only a few instances has a curb been found, which set the orchestra apart from the line of the gutter and the seats; e.g., at Epidauros, Oiniadai, Corinth, and Argos, large theaters where the orchestra had become a distinct, decorative element.

12. Vitruvius introduces his description of theater construction with the finding of a suitable location, preferably on a hillside (*De Architectura*, v. 3. 3). Next, he begins the plan of both the Greek and Roman theater with a basic circle *(perimetros)* that determined the location of the first row of seats (v. 6. 1; 7. 1). Even Vitruvius does not distinguish between an orchestra circle and the curve of the cavea, which he further elaborates.

In earlier times, some other planning procedure may well have been in use. S. Ferri in his commentary on Vitruvius (*De Architectura*, trans. with notes by S. Ferri [Rome: Palombi, 1960], pp. 190 ff.) cites the peculiar system of inscribing a polygon in the basic circle to determine the other parts of a Greek or Roman theater when the circle alone would have been sufficient. He continues: "There were evidently two structural concepts of a different origin and chronology, one a circular [concept] and one a polygonal." Beginning from the premise that circular choral dances gave rise to a circular orchestra, which was then enclosed by a trapezoidal cavea of wood, he suggests that the late fifth and fourth century theories on acoustics and harmonics and the Pythagorean idea of the harmony of celestial spheres led to the introduction of a curvilinear cavea. He concludes with the idea that when the architect tried to reconcile the straight front of the skene with a curved cavea he resorted to the current geometric figure of squaring a circle, which is still echoed in the Vitruvian system.

It would be simpler and perhaps more correct, however, to suggest that when the architect started to plan a curved cavea, very likely under the influence of contemporary theories on acoustics as well as for reasons of improved visibility, he began with the square base that he had been accustomed to use in laying out a straight or trapezoidal-shaped cavea with a skene opposite it. He then enclosed that square with a circle and added more polygonal figures as needed. It is noteworthy that even in Vitruvius the location for the front of the proskenion

At present the gutter alone is left to indicate what form the cavea at Isthmia originally took: two straight wings diverge slightly toward the skene, and very likely they were connected by a straight center section.[13] A similar arrangement may be found in the early rock-cut theater at Syracuse where, also, only the gutter channels remain to mark the line of what may have been a three-sided cavea and orchestra.[14] The channels, measuring about 0.40 m to 0.60 m in width, correspond to nothing in the later Greek or Roman caveas; they lie at a higher level than the other gutters and were perhaps walled up when the first curved gutter was cut.[15] On the sides they resemble the southern extension of the channels at Isthmia, although there is nothing at Syracuse comparable to the northern part that was never used. The theater at Syracuse was reportedly designed by Damocopos in the fifth century B.C. and would have continued in use until

is determined by the basic square that is on the central axis and may represent the original figure of the early theater plan.

A detailed examination of the acoustical properties of both rectilinear and curved caveas has been carried out by F. Canac (*L'Acoustique des Théâtres Antiques, ses Enseignements* [Paris: Editions du Centre National de la Recherche Scientifique, 1967], pp. 69 ff.).

13. The traditional and prevailing view concerning the early Greek theater identifies an orchestra circle as the first and basic element around which seats, gutter, and skene were arranged. It received archaeological impetus from the remains in the Theater of Dionysos at Athens, which Dörpfeld interpreted as marking the edge of the early orchestra circle, and henceforth the orchestra circle has been taken as axiomatic for almost all other Greek theaters; see Dörpfeld, *Gr. Th.*, pp. 26–36. Summaries of subsequent discussion are found in Bieber, *Greek and Roman Theater*, pp. 54–64, n. 7; W. Dinsmoor, "The Athenian Theater of the Fifth Century," *Studies Presented to David M. Robinson* (2 vols.; Saint Louis: Washington University Press, 1951), 1: 310–14. The problem of the evidence for this early orchestra at Athens is too involved to be explored here (see Preface, pp. xv–xvii), but for the cavea there are remains that indicate that it was constructed with straight rows of seats. Seat blocks and foundations (perhaps for a wooden proedria), dated by inscriptions on them to near the end of the fifth century, have been found reused in the later theater; see H. Bulle, *Untersuchungen an griechischen Theatern*, Vol. 33 of the *Abhandlungen der bayerischen Akademie der Wissenschaften* (Munich: R. Oldenbourg, 1928), 56–70, Pl. 6, Figs. 8–11, Pl. 7; and O. Dilke, "The Greek Theatre Cavea," *BSA* 43 (1948): 165–66. The absence of any curve on the blocks led even Dinsmoor to reconstruct a polygonal cavea, although he manages to bend it around a circular orchestra (*Studies* 1: 328–29, Figs. 2–3).

In other theaters outside of Athens, which are of early date or simple plan, there is no trace of an orchestra circle, and the seats were clearly arranged in straight rows. Notwithstanding that all extant caveas belong to the time of stone construction, the straight examples undoubtedly reflect an earlier type of seating in wood, which by its nature would have been laid out in straight segments; see Dilke, *BSA* 43 (1948): 127, 146–53. The orchestra in turn would have been the level open area at the foot of the seats, bounded by the front of the skene at the other side, and so essentially quadrilateral in shape. At Tegea a paved walk, gutter, and stone curb (presumably bordering the orchestra, which has not been excavated) follow the straight line of the seats. This is the best example of a formal unity between the proedria, gutter, and orchestra curb since all elements are represented and preserved. A straight row of proedria thrones also existed at Rhamnous and Ikaria. At Thorikos the cavea has a straight center section ending in curved wings that may have been an innovation to increase seating capacity and visibility. These theaters are currently assigned to the fourth century B.C. with

Hieron II (270–216 B.C.) built the large stone structure that is still visible.[16] At Cyrene another rock-cut theater preserves rectangular cuttings in the cavea that seem to indicate that a trapezoidal seating arrangement there, too, preceded the large, curved auditorium.[17] The early theatron at Argos beneath the Roman odeion[18] and the theater at Thorikos were rectilinear with curved wings. The theater at Corinth is particularly relevant to Isthmia because of its proximity and the control that the large urban center exerted over the Sanctuary. The late-fourth century B.C. curb system in the orchestra exhibits a strange combination of curved and trapezoidal elements reminiscent of the trapezoidal orchestra at Syracuse, which was

the exception of Thorikos where recent excavations have revealed that the first retaining wall (A-A) at the rear of the orchestra goes back to the end of the sixth century; T. Hackens, *Thorikos 1965* 3 (1967): 80–95, Fig. 114, Plan V; ibid., "Thorikos 1963: Le Théâtre," *L'Antiquité Classique* 34 (1965): 44, 45. The orchestra was enlarged in the mid-fifth century by the addition of a second retaining wall (B-B), and Hackens suggests that the stone seats of the lower cavea were constructed at that time. The first seats, contemporary with the early orchestra, would have probably been of wood. The first theater at Morgantina, Sicily, has also been found to have had straight rows of seats, perhaps arranged in a trapezoidal form. Several rows are preserved from what appears to have been the upper section of one wing; none have been found in probes at lower levels, perhaps because they were destroyed when the later, curved auditorium was cut more deeply into the hill. The theater was initially constructed about 325 B.C. (H. Allen, "Excavations at Morgantina, 1967–1969, Preliminary Report X," *AJA* 74 [1970]: 363–64).

14. Anti, *Teatri Greci Arcaici*, pp. 98 ff., Pl. VII. Much in this book has been challenged. Dinsmoor accepted the reconstruction of a trapezoidal orchestra and cavea at Syracuse (*AAG*, p. 210); more recently, Bernabo Brea has restudied the remains and returns to Rizzo's conclusion that the trapezoidal channels belong to a late Roman hydraulic system (L. Bernabo Brea, "Studi sul teatro greco di Siracusa," *Palladio* 17 [1967]: 97–98, 114–15, 146 ff., Fig. 78); G. Rizzo, *Il Teatro Greco di Siracusa* (Milan: Bestetti and Tumminelli, 1923), 143, Figs. 10, 14, Pls. I, III. Bernabo Brea includes an extensive bibliography on the theater. He argues that if there had been an earlier theater on the site, the recutting of the seats would have removed all trace of it; and no cavea smaller than the present one would have been cut so deeply into the rock of the hillside. The remains themselves, largely rock-cut, are difficult to interpret. Yet, in other theaters recutting of seats has not obliterated cuttings in the orchestra. His reconstructions of the first and second phases of the orchestra (Figs. 36, 40) seem strangely out of harmony with the great sweep of the cavea, especially the wings of the first gutter that diverge in an odd, trapezoidal fashion, and the removal of seats at the sides of the cavea of the second period seems unusual in a Hellenistic theater. A large-scale actual state plan of the remains and smaller detailed drawings are needed to begin to understand the problems of the site.

15. A section taken on the vertical axis would be helpful to see the levels in the orchestra, the cavea, and between the various water channels.

16. Anti, *Teatri Greci Arcaici*, pp. 103–6; Dinsmoor, *AAG*, pp. 210, 299, n. 4.

17. Anti (*Teatri Greci Arcaici*, pp. 122–25) and G. Caputo ("Note sugli edifici teatrali della Cirenaica," in *Anthemon* [Florence: G. C. Sansoni. 1955], p. 282) suggest a fifth-century date for the early theater on the basis of historical probability, but without evidence from excavation.

18. G. Roux reports that the rock-cut seats curve slightly at the ends, especially at the north, probably resulting from irregularities of the hillside. An accurate plan of the cuttings is now in preparation; see G. Roux, "Chronique des Fouilles en 1955: Argos," *BCH* 80 (1956): 395–96.

a colony of Corinth. It may be that the Corinth theater in the fifth century had a three-sided cavea and orchestra that in turn influenced the plan adopted at Isthmia and finally left its imprint on the elaborate curb design of the following period.[19]

In summary, some theaters (see n. 13) were designed with straight rows of seats; those at Syracuse, Cyrene, Thorikos, and Argos combined a straight center section with straight or curved wings at the sides. At Athens and Morgantina the arrangement is not clear, but trapezoidal is more probable, and the theater at Isthmia is now added to the second group.

The Skene

The vertical scarp at the north side of the orchestra is composed of clay on the east side and, on the west, of silt deposited by the stream that ran down the hill in prehistoric times. Because of the crumbly nature of the scarp, a retaining wall would have been required as soon as the cavea and orchestra were hollowed out of the hillside, and the wall probably ran in approximately the same line as the later ashlar wall (between points (a) and (b) on Pl. I). This is one feature of the early theater about which there can be a fair degree of certainty because of the exigencies imposed by a sunken orchestra. As soon as the unprotected scarp was again laid bare during the excavations of 1959–62, the clay began to flake off to such a degree that a modern retaining wall had to be built along the east side where the top is unprotected by Roman masonry.

Another feature that may be assigned to the early skene is a floor surface

19. The resemblance between the trapezoidal elements at Corinth and Syracuse has been noted by Dinsmoor (*AAG*, p. 314); R. Stillwell (*The Theatre*, Vol. 2 of *Corinth: Results of the Excavations Conducted by the American School of Classical Studies at Athens* [Princeton: American School of Classical Studies at Athens, 1952]: 133) denies there is any connection between them. Furthermore, the date of about 415 B.C. assigned to the large curved auditorium p. 131) is open to revision on the basis of bronze coins of the Pegasus and Trident series found in connection with the few remaining seat blocks, stairways, and their foundations; see T. Shear, "Excavations in the Theatre District and Tombs of Corinth in 1929," *AJA* 33 (1929): 517–18. M. Price, in a forthcoming work on Corinthian coinage, places the beginning of this series close to 365/60 B.C., and the coins from the theater appear to belong to the years 330/303 B.C. according to his chronology. He further notes that no issue of bronze coinage on the mainland can be dated earlier than 410/400 B.C. Further evidence awaits excavation of the final two-thirds of the cavea, which certainly is fourth century.

The inscriptions on the seat blocks might also be helpful, but they have been variously assigned to the early fifth century, later fifth century, and early fourth century (cf. Stillwell, *The Theatre*, pp. 110, nos. 41–49, 131; Fig. 86; J. Kent, *The inscriptions, 1926–1950*, Vol. 8, Pt. 3, of *Corinth: Results of the Excavations Conducted by the American School of Classical Studies at Athens* [Princeton: The American School of Classical Studies at Athens, 1966]: 4, no. 11; 5, no. 16; 6, nos. 18, 19, 20; Pl. 2). As Stillwell points out, ". . . thus far we do not have sufficient knowledge of Corinthian epigraphy to be positive."

Yet another indication of an earlier cavea is the location of the postholes assigned to the early skene, the axis of which is about 3.40 m east of the central axis of the curved auditorium; see Stillwell, *The Theatre*, pp. 32–33, Pls. III, IV.

with tiny pebbles embedded in it inside the area of the later proskenion. The preserved portion is on the west side beginning at the central passage and continuing without interruption under the first three rectangular bases and appearing again at the northwest corner of the proskenion. The floor is 0.83 to 0.90 m wide from the ashlar retaining wall to its south edge where it ends in a straight line, except for a jog near the west end (Fig. 9). The surface is at a level of −0.09 to −0.14 m, sloping gradually down toward the west. No sign of the pebble surface can be distinguished on the east side where the native clay is higher and the floor would not have been as well marked.[20]

The pebble floor may be securely assigned to the first period of the theater because it lies 0.09 to 0.14 m below the floor of the proskenion in later Greek periods (chap. 2, pp. 42, 53) and the floor level in Roman times was even higher.

From the way in which the pebble floor ends in a straight line along its

20. A row of small stones was found on the east side in line with the south edge of the pebble floor on the west (Pl. I). Along the north side of the stones a rectangular cutting (2.00 m by 0.72 m) continues as far back as the retaining wall for the scarp and would have included the entire width of the pebble floor. The function and date of the stones and cutting remain obscure except that the earth in the bottom of the cutting contained sherds of early Roman date.

Fig. 9. Pebble floor inside the proskenion of the first Greek period. Fallen sun-baked bricks at right along the edge of the floor. At top, ashlar retaining wall for scarp, looking north.

Fig. 10. Central passage, east side; stair shaft of first Greek period at left end. Note sloping south edge (right side) marked with arrow.

Fig. 11. East end of the proskenion, looking northeast. Arrow marks cutting (b) for east end of first proskenion.

south edge, it seems likely that it originally came to a stop against a wall or foundation for supports, parallel to the retaining wall. A narrow porch would thus have been formed along the face of the scarp. If the front section was a solid wall, undoubtedly there would have been a door in the center and possibly side openings as well; otherwise, there may have been wooden supports at regular intervals on a stylobate, in the nature of a porch. Fragments of sun-dried bricks that were found along the edge of the floor and in the central passage may have come from a front wall or from the retaining wall for the scarp (Figs. 9, 10, 11).[21] It is significant that the passage, although only about 0.90 m wide, stood in approximately the same position and general relationship to the skene as the normal prokenion of the later Greek periods.[22] In the literal sense of the word it was "that which stood in front of the skene". Surely of light construction and perhaps of a removable nature, it served the same purpose as the later proskenion by providing mobility for the performers in their entrances and exits from the orchestra and a platform for solo performances.[23] The sunken orchestra made construction of rooms difficult at the lower level, and without the proskenion entrance to the orchestra from the skene would have been very limited.

Cuttings in clay outside the end walls of the later proskenion mark the limits of the first proskenion (Pl. I at (a) and (b)). They slant in toward the orchestra at approximately the same angle and orientation as the gutter channels on each side (Fig. 11 shows the east side; an arrow marks the edge). The correspondence seems to be close enough to associate the slanted cuttings with the early period. At present they stop slightly south

21. All the fragments are about 0.08 m thick. Brick fragments were also found just north and west of the center of the proskenion sill and toward the north end of the central passage. Cf. the early theater at Eretria, the skene of which seems to have been constructed with unbaked bricks in the second half of the fifth century (Bulle, *Untersuchungen an griechischen Theatern*, pp. 85–87; E. Fiechter, *Das Theater in Eretria*, Vol. 8 of *Antike griechische Theaterbauten* [Stuttgart: W. Kohlhammer, 1937]: 10, 13, 34). The theater at Babylon was also made of mud-bricks in the fourth century (Bulle, p. 246; Dinsmoor, *AAG*, p. 304). See the discussion of brick construction in R. Martin, *Matériaux et Techniques*, part I of *Manuel d'Architecture Grecque* (Paris: A. and J. Picard, 1965), pp. 46–57. He notes that the majority of bricks have a thickness of about 0.08 m; parts of the gymnasium at Epidauros and the palaestra at Olympia were of this construction.

22. The roof of the passage would have projected about 0.10 m at the front and was probably finished with a molding, so that the actual width of about 1 m on top would have been sufficient for a performer to stand on, if desired.

23. Dinsmoor points out that in theaters with a sunken orchestra a proskenion was necessary to allow the actors to circulate without being seen by the audience (*AAG*, p. 300). Although he used this reasoning to prove that no permanent proskenion was built before the third century B.C., nevertheless it holds true for the Isthmian theater from the beginning where the simple proskenion was not only a decorative addition but a functional necessity. It is interesting that the first theater at Eretria may have had porches about 1 m wide on the first floor along the inside of the paraskenia, according to Bulle (*Untersuchungen an griechischen Theatern*, p. 86). Fiechter disagrees (*Ant. Th.* 8: 13).

of the pebble floor and probably ended there, even with the front of the proskenion.[24]

A passage on the central axis at orchestra level also must have been cut through the scarp at this period. A small section of its pebble floor was found at the south end of the passage, 0.29 m below the second Greek floor level. Most of the floor would have been destroyed when the central drain was laid. The several fragments of sun-dried bricks that were found farther north beneath the later floor probably came from the retaining walls lining the passage (Fig. 12, d). Two rectangular cuttings in the clay

24. See the theater at Ikaria where the ends of the retaining wall at the rear of the orchestra terrace turn and diverge toward the proedria.

Fig. 12. Central passage, center section, looking west. At the top is the west wall (a), center is the central drain with cover slabs (b), below is the hard floor of the first Roman period (c), and thin *stroses* beneath it exposed to the left. Lower center is a fallen sun-baked brick (d).

scarp of the east side, about 1.00 m above hardpan, very likely received wooden members that were part of the framework of the brick wall (Fig. 10). A posthole in the passage floor (0.28 m in diameter and 0.18 m deep) may also have held a post to support the wall.

At the northeast corner of the passage a vertical shaft was cut through the clay with an oblique entrance from the passage (Pl. I, Fig. 10). The main (south) section of the shaft is rectangular, 1.03 m by 0.70 m; including the oblique opening at the north, it has a total length of 1.80 m (north-south) and a width of 1.30 m. The southern scarp of the shaft inclines toward the south a maximum of 0.27 m from the vertical measured at the top (Fig. 10, arrow), and the shaft is at present 1.50 m deep.

The shaft could have accommodated a small, ladderlike stairway on the sloping south side, which would have connected the skene on top of the scarp with the passage and the orchestra. A few third-century B.C. sherds found in the fill inside lead to the supposition that the stair continued to be used into the following period. At the north end the central passage ended without access to the outside or there was a short flight of stairs, as in succeeding periods.

Although nothing remains of a scene-building on top of the clay bank, it is reasonable to suppose that some kind of building stood there. The stair-shaft needed an upper terminus, and the narrow proskenion at orchestra level would not have been large enough to serve as skene. The building would have been of wood, perhaps a temporary structure erected every two years at the time of the festival. Its dimensions very likely corresponded approximately to the skene-building of the following period (Pl. IV): the length equal to the proskenion and the width matching the extent of the central passage.

A cutting in the clay on top of the bank, located inside room I of the Roman scene-building, should be related to this period. It measures 1.05 m by 1.25 m and is 0.43 m deep (Pl. I). The top of the cutting was filled with a solid layer of clay, and below it were broken pieces of clay, reddish earth, and a few sherds of pre-Roman date. This is similar to the material found in other cuttings (at the ends of the proskenion and the shaft at the north end of the central passage) discontinued about the end of the period, and the rectangular cutting may have been filled in at the same time. Similar, though larger, cuttings are found in the theater of Eretria where they appear to have received foundations for theatrical machinery.[25]

One final feature must be included in our description of the first period of the theater: a cistern lay north of the scene-building in the center of the area that later became the court. Only a small portion of it has been uncovered, including what appears to be its northern edge located about

25. See Fiechter, *Ant. Th.* 8: 15.

23

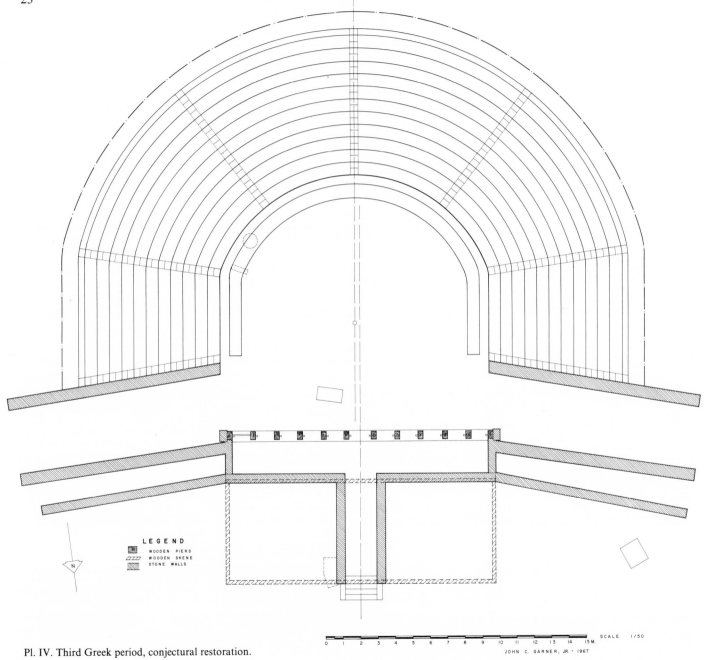

LEGEND
WOODEN PIERS
WOODEN SKENE
STONE WALLS

N

SCALE 1/50

0 1 2 3 4 5 6 7 8 9 10 11 12 13 14 15 M.

JOHN C. GARNER, JR. - 1967

Pl. IV. Third Greek period, conjectural restoration.

8.30 m from the north side of the court.[26] The floor is made of hard, heavy brown stucco, and many pieces broken from its sides were found in the earth inside. That its collapse took place around the middle of the fourth century B.C. can be deduced from the fact that none of the pottery seems to be of a definitely later date except for a few fragments of coarse Roman ware. This contamination may have resulted from the laying of the central drain across the area in the first century A.D. Additional information about the cistern and its connection, if any, with the water system of the early theater must await further excavation.

Chronology

Nothing was found in the theater to reveal the date of its initial construction, but some indication of the end of the first period is given by the pottery found in the bottom of manholes 1 and 2 and in the silt in the underground drain itself.[27] The fragments of pottery, for the most part, are of coarse fabric and common shape, a few of them almost whole, typical of the fifth and fourth centuries B.C.[28] More closely identifiable, however, is a small round vessel, 0.072 m in diameter and 0.023 m high, with concave sides, light buff fabric, and covered inside and out with black glaze (IP 2844, Fig. 13). This type of vessel, called a saltcellar, was first made in the late fifth century B.C. and continued to be made until the mid-

26. The presence of the cistern was detected during the spring campaign of 1967, but time allowed for only a small trial trench that included a section of the central drain. A tunnel was extended about 3.50 m toward the south in an unsuccessful attempt to find the edge of the cistern. G. Roger Edwards kindly examined the pottery from the cistern and supplied the information concerning its date.

27. Although all of the manholes were opened in later times, the bulk of the material is coarse Greek ware and the bottom of the deposit was undisturbed.

28. The pottery shapes from the drain included pitchers, two-handled cooking pots, and a wide-brimmed lekane. I am much indebted to G. Roger Edwards, Brian Sparks, and D. A. Amyx for their expert opinion on the dates of the vases from the drain and the theater caves. Mr. Amyx supplied the dimensions for pieces (b) and (c) in the catalogue.

Fig. 13. Small black-glazed bowl (IP 2846) and "saltcellar" (IP 2844) from underground drain of first Greek period.

IP 2846   IP 2844

Fig. 14. Two-handled jug (IP 2843) from underground drain of first Greek period.

Fig. 15. Inscribed sherd (IP 2827) from underground drain of first Greek period.

Fig. 16. Two eaves-tiles (IA 662, 704) from manhole 1 of the first Greek period.

fourth century B.C.; the present example is dated (by Brian Sparks) near the end of that time in view of its high waistline.[29]

Other vases and objects worthy of mention in connection with the drain are the following:

(a) Two-handled pitcher or Corinthian decanter (IP 2843, Fig. 14)
Max. diam. 0.150 m, height 0.169 m.
Light buff fabric undecorated except for two horizontal bands painted around the shoulder. It has a slightly projecting lip and small ring base. It resembles others of a slightly different profile and is assigned (by G. Roger Edwards) to the second quarter of the fourth century B.C.[30]

(b) Black-painted skyphos bottom (IP 2825)
Max. ht. 0.050 m, diam. of base 0.055 m.
It is dated (by Mr. Edwards) to the third quarter of the fourth century B.C.

(c) Kantharos fragment (IP 2835)
Max. ht. 0.055 m, max. width 0.065 m.
Black and brown colored glaze on the outside, brown on the inside. Assigned to the fourth century B.C.

(d) Inscribed sherd (IP 2827, Fig. 15)
Max. ht. 0.120 m, max. width 0.08 m.
The letters are incised in horizontal, parallel lines and are fairly uniform in size. Both sides of the graffito are apparently broken off, and damage to the surface makes decipherment difficult. The letter forms appear to be from the second half of the fourth century B.C.[31]

(e) Two painted terra-cotta eaves-tiles (IA 662, IA 704, Fig. 16)
Light buff clay, apparently of Corinthian manufacture. The outer edge is decorated with checkered squares connected by a meander; the under portion has a reserved bead and reel. They do not come from the same roof, but are very similar and belong to the fourth century.[32]
The filling up of the drain, then, falls in the second half of the fourth

29. The saltcellar is similar to examples found at Olynthus (D. M. Robinson, *Mosaics, Vases, and Lamps of Olynthus*, Vol. 5 of *Excavations at Olynthus* [14 vols.; Baltimore: Johns Hopkins Press, 1933]: 253, no. 142, Pl. 189; D. M. Robinson, *Vases Found in 1934 and 1938*. Vol. 13 of ibid. [1950]: Pls. 232, 238, 239). See P. Corbett, "Attic Pottery of the Later Fifth Century from the Athenian Agora," *Hesperia* 18 (1949): 329–30, no. 68, Pl. 93.

30. Cf. Corbett, *Hesperia* 18 (1949): 345, no. 165, Pl. 96; M. Pease, "A Well of the Late Fifth Century at Corinth," *Hesperia* 6 (1937): 294, no. 151, Fig. 25.

31. Michael Jameson, who is studying the inscriptions from Isthmia, supplied information concerning the date, but the meaning is obscure. It may be a list of proper names.

32. Cf. O. Broneer, *The South Stoa and Its Roman Successors*, Vol. 1, Pt. 4 of *Corinth: Results of the Excavations Conducted by the American School of Classical Studies at Athens* (Princeton: The American School of Classical Studies at Athens, 1954): Pl. 20 (4) top. The design is similiar.

century; but it is difficult to be more precise. The vases found in the kitchen of the theater cave[33] closely resemble those from the underground drain and the Rachi settlement,[34] and they are dated (by G. Roger Edwards) to the years around 350 B.C. However, inasmuch as Hellenistic sherds occurred inside the bedding for the stone border around the second orchestra (chap. 2, p. 36), the remodeling of the cavea and orchestra at the end of the first Greek period is best placed near the end of the century.

The initial construction of the theater would have taken place some years earlier, perhaps around 400 B.C. In 390 B.C. a fire severely damaged the columns and roof of the Temple of Poseidon, and extensive repairs were necessary to return the temple to its original condition.[35] Probably as a consequence, the years following the disaster seem to have been uneventful ones with no evidence of new buildings; the repairs to the temple had first priority. It was not until the middle of the century that prosperity returned: a settlement was established on the Rachi,[36] and a new stadium replaced the old.[37] Consequently, in view of the fire and the subsequent decline in building activity at Isthmia, the date of the first theater is more apt to fit into the history of the sanctuary before 390 B.C. than in the years immediately following.

33. Broneer, *Hesperia* 31 (1962): 6–7, Pl. 12a-e and Broneer, *Isthmia II*, in press.

34. C. Kardara, "Dyeing and Weaving Works at Isthmia," *AJA* 65 (1961): 261–66, Pl. 82, Figs. 9, 10, 13, 14.

35. O. Broneer, "The Temple of Poseidon at Isthmia," Χαριστήριον εἰς Ἀναστάσιον Κ. Ὀρλάνδον (4 vols.; Athens: Ἀρχαιολογικὴ Ἑταιρεῖα, 1965–68), 3: 65–66; O. Broneer, *Isthmia I: The Temple of Poseidon* (Princeton: The American School of Classical Studies at Athens, 1971), pp. 101–2.

36. Kardara, *AJA* 65 (1961): 263. She dates the beginning of the Rachi settlement to about 360 B.C.

37. Broneer, *Hesperia* 31 (1962): 12–13.

2

The Second and Third Greek Periods

The avid interest in theater construction that pervaded Greece in the second half of the fourth century B.C. spread also to Isthmia. The old three-sided cavea and orchestra must have appeared antiquated at a time when the curved form had been widely adopted as its advantages for the spectator became evident. It was time that the theater be remodeled in accordance with a curvilinear plan. The cavea required a complete re-cutting that, in turn, gave the orchestra a new outline. In addition a new scene-building was constructed with a larger proskenion.

The Cavea

The present curved cavea dates from another remodeling of the first Roman period, but a few traces of its predecessor remain. The upper edge of the Greek seats would have corresponded roughly with the top of the Roman seat-cuttings (+2.52 m) because the hill levels off abruptly above that line and, except for the T-shaped piers of the second Roman period, there are no traces of heavy foundations that could have supported an upper extension of the cavea in stone. Any additional seating would have been in the nature of wooden bleachers *(ikria)*, erected when the size of the crowd warranted it. Most of the time the overflow very likely sat on the bare hillside, as they regularly did in the later stadium.[1]

The lower limit of the cavea extended about 2.50 m farther into the orchestra than the present one does, as measured from the ends of the analemmata represented by Block E and cutting F (Pls. I, III, Fig. 18) which are described below, p. 30. Thus, the incline of the seats with a rise of 1 m in 3.20 m would not have been as steep as that of its Roman successor, which was 1 m in 2.72 m.[2] On the assumption that each row (including seat and footrest) was about 0.70 m wide, there would have been room for twelve rows of seats with a walk about 0.95 m wide behind the twelfth row, which would have been in the nature of a diazoma of packed

1. O. Broneer, "Excavations at Isthmia, 1959-1961," *Hesperia* 31 (1962): 11.
2. This is based on a total depth of 9.00 m for the Greek cavea, measured on the axis. The rise is even more gradual than that found at Corinth, which is 1:3.06 for the Greek period; R. Stillwell, *The Theatre*, Vol. 2 of *Corinth: Results of the Excavations Conducted by the American School of Classical Studies at Athens* (Princeton: The American School of Classical Studies at Athens, 1952), p. 26.

Fig. 17. Restored section of second Greek period.

clay. With a total rise of 2.52 m, the actual clay foundations for the seat blocks would have had a height of about 0.21 m. In this type of theater, construction of the seats themselves was probably quite simple, perhaps rectangular stone blocks with earth packed behind them to form the foot-rests slightly lower than the seats, as in the theater at Corinth.[3] Spectators in the first row very likely used the packed earth section inside the paved walk (below, p. 39) for a footrest.

The absence of the actual seat foundations from this period precludes any positive restoration of the stairways. A possible arrangement is given on the restored plan (Pl. IV). The cavea would have been divided into six sections by seven stairways, each about 0.45 m wide.[4] The arrangement in the section where the curved portion of the seats met the straight wings is particularly uncertain, although a stair has been indicated on the plan.

The seating capacity of the lower cavea can be estimated on the basis of twelve rows of permanent seats. With a space of 0.36 m allotted for each spectator as at Corinth, approximately 1,550 persons could have been accommodated, with room for many more on the slope above.

The ends of the analemmata of the cavea are represented by a limestone block (E) on the west side and a cutting (F) for a similar block on the east. The remainder of the walls on both sides has been removed and the beddings obscured by Roman construction. Block E and cutting F mark the lower limits of the analemmata and give the line of the walls that came in at a more pronounced angle with respect to the skene than the Roman walls (Fig. 18).[5]

Block E is hard limestone, 1.63 m by 0.65 m and 0.50 m high, roughly finished on three sides and perhaps broken at the west end. Two shifting notches close together at the east attest the presence of a second course,

3. Ibid., pp. 22–24, Fig. 13. The rectangular seat blocks are 0.30 m high and 0.37 m wide. From the restored drawings in Figs. 13 and 18, based on the remains, the total width of the rows was about 0.70 m. A drafting at the rear of the seat blocks indicates that the footrest was about 0.02 m–0.04 m below the seat. A similar kind of disconnected seating is found at Eretria and in the stadia at Olympia and Epidauros; see O. Dilke, "The Greek Theatre Cavea," *BSA* 43 (1948): 158–60, Figs. 19–20. It also appears at Leontion and in the three straight rows of seats recently discovered in the theater at Morgantina.

4. This is narrow for stairways, which usually range between 0.60 m and 0.90 m in width, but compare the theater on Thera where they have a width of only 0.30 m; O. Dilke, "Details and Chronology of Greek Theatre Caveas," *BSA* 45 (1950): 60. The narrow stairs at Isthmia, at least along the outer edges of the end *kerkides*, are suggested by the fact that the stone border around the orchestra stops about 0.42 m short of the outer retaining wall, and it would have been awkward to have it end halfway across the entrance to a stairway.

5. The term analemma (pl. analemmata) will be used throughout to designate the retaining wall at each end of the cavea. In Greek theaters generally, the analemmata diverged from the line of the skene as they approached the orchestra, while the walls of Roman caveas were usually parallel to the scene-building, or nearly so. The orientation of the Roman analemmata here differs from that of the Greek in a direction more nearly parallel to the scene-building.

Fig. 18. West half of orchestra and west parodos,
looking west. Block E (arrow) and foundation for
Ionic column of second Roman period in foreground.

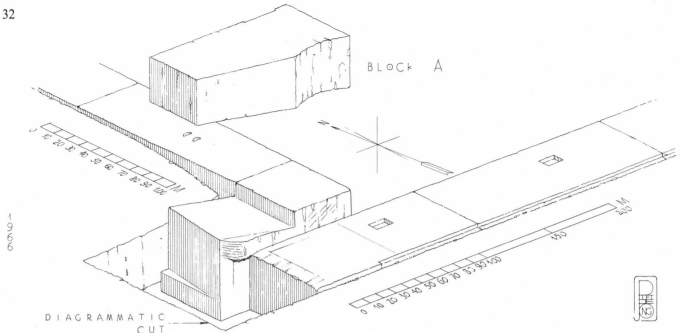

BLOCK A

Pl. V. Restored isometric detail of the west end of the proskenion sill.

and the sloping top surface indicates that the first course, at least, followed the slope of the parodos floor in the same manner as the north parodos wall opposite it (Pl. V). The east face of E, perpendicular to the skene and more carefully finished than the others with a flat chisel, was probably cut after the block was in place so that it followed exactly the line planned for the edge of the orchestra. In Roman times the next block west of E also remained in place, as was the case with the two corresponding blocks on the east side.[6]

The Orchestra

The orchestra was of necessity reshaped at the time of the construction of a new cavea. A stone walk replaced the water channels at the sides, and manhole 1 was put out of operation by a hard-packed filling of large stones and earth that contained some pottery (chap. 1, pp. 24–26).

Although the orchestra floor from this period is not preserved (chap. 4,

6. Probably because they were not conspicuous and may have served some useful purpose; see chap. 3, p. 72.

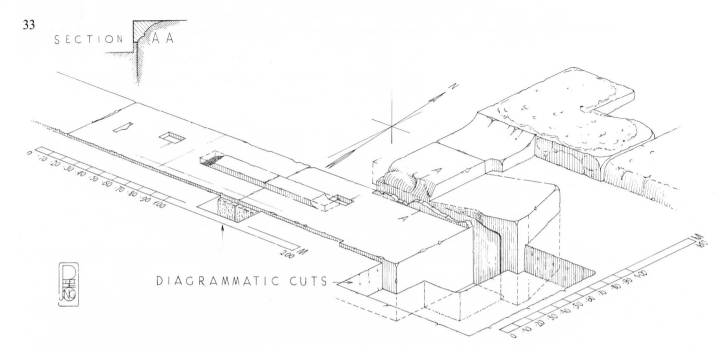

SECTION A A

DIAGRAMMATIC CUTS

Pl. VI. Isometric detail of the east end of the proskenion sill.

pp. 134–35), a close estimate of its level can be made. The top of block E (east end) reaches to $+0.05$ m, which must have been at ground level or below because even the east face of the block is so roughly finished that it could never have been intended to be seen.[7] On the other hand the floor could not have been much higher than $+0.05$ m because the highest point of the first proskenion sill was $+0.07$ m (p. 50). Thus, the orchestra floor would have lain between $+0.05$ m and $+0.07$ m (Fig.18) and it would have been fairly level, inasmuch as the closing of the manhole would have eliminated the need for a slope in that direction.[8]

A few cuttings in hardpan mark the edge of the orchestra floor. They appear to have been made in connection with a stone border probably used as a walk, although the perishable nature of the clay and later reconstructions make a precise restoration impossible. Excavation of the area was

7. Compare with the smooth finishing of the west wall of the central passage that was exposed to view (Fig. 26).
8. On the present proskenion sill a rebate 0.04 m high along its front edge indicates that the orchestra floor may have sloped down to -0.04 m along the proskenion, at least by the time of the stone sill.

Fig. 19. The theater, looking west from the east side, storeroom in the foreground.

Fig. 20. The orchestra, looking west. Manhole 1 and block G in center foreground; bedding for walk at edge of second Greek orchestra cut into early channel at lower right; trenches to expose cuttings for the edge of the second Greek orchestra around remainder of orchestra.

undertaken with all possible care and by means of small trenches, and all cuttings and trenches together with elevations in terms of the zero point at the east end of the proskenion sill are shown on the actual state plan (Pl. III, Figs. 1, 20).[9]

The central section of the orchestra bed, at a level of about −0.38 m to −0.41 m, was covered with a layer of fine clay that was very likely added at the time that the orchestra was cut in the first period, in order to fill deep holes and grooves in the hardpan. Probably at the same time the bed was given a slope to the south. Virgin clay is found at a level of −0.12 m immediately south of the proskenion sill, and about 4.50 m farther south it descends fairly rapidly to about −0.38 m. As noted above, the actual orchestra floor in the second period would have been approximately level with the proskenion sill.

The best preserved section of the border cutting at the edge of the orchestra is found along the east side, area (a) (Pl. III, Figs. 1, 6), where both edges of a long straight bedding are visible. The bedding, about 0.09 m deep, lies at right angles to the proskenion sill and stretches southward for 4.76 m, coming to an end at block G. It varies in width between 0.65 m and 0.74 m due to the irregularity of the clay, and the bottom (−0.51 m to −0.52 m) is pocked with grooves and hollows filled with earth. The bedding is cut into the eastern edge of the early orchestra channel so that there is no doubt but that it is later than the drainage channel.

Just before it reaches block G, the bedding begins a slight curve inward, and the block appears to mark the commencement of the curved portion of the orchestra. The limestone block (0.85 m by 0.25 m), set deep into the clay, served as a foundation block, and on its top surface at the east end is a pry hole cut to move a block toward the north (Fig. 6). It perhaps carried the final block of the stone border that would have defined the straight east side of the orchestra, inasmuch as the clay bedding was filled with a packing of earth equal in height to block G and slightly overlapping it; the blocks of the border would have rested on that. They would have been about 0.54 m high in order to equal the level of the orchestra floor and project slightly above it.

South of block G, manhole 1 of the early drain falls in the line where a continuation of the bedding would be expected, but no trace of a cutting

9. The border of the orchestra is divided for convenience into areas lettered (a) through (g), beginning at the east end. The eastern portion (area a) and almost half of the center section (b) were cleared to virgin clay in 1962, as well as the area between (g) and block E. The remainder was uncovered in 1967. Many sections of the packing that originally filled the cutting have been left as markers and may be distinguished from the surrounding clay by their stony surface. All of the levels on Pl. III are expressed to the third decimal place, but in the description in the text levels are rounded off to two decimal places.

was found. Although the manhole was not open at the time, some kind of stone covering was undoubtedly provided and the border of the orchestra would have passed over it. The whole area of the manhole and south of it is badly eroded and full of deep holes and grooves (Fig. 1).[10]

The central section of the preserved bedding begins about 4.70 m southwest of the manhole (west end of area b, Pl. III)[11] and continues around the south end of the orchestra and up the west side for a total of about 5 m (through area e). Only the inner edge is without interruption; the outer line is missing in area (b) but it appears again in (c) through (e), giving the bedding a width of 0.76 m. On the axis of the orchestra there is a roughly rectangular cutting (0.94 m by 0.28 to 0.40 m) sunk 0.13 m below the bottom of the bedding. It was filled to the bottom with a packing of earth, pieces of clay, and poros chips in which there was a sherd of the fifth century B.C., a Greek roof-tile fragment, and some pieces of Greek cement. What purpose it served is not clear.

The entire section (b) through (e) was covered on top by a layer of packing composed of poros chips, earth, and clay. It begins at a level of −0.35 m to −0.43 m and continues down to a lower level of clay fill at −0.42 m to −0.48 m (Figs. 21 and 22 show the difference between the two layers). Very few sherds were found in either layer of packing, and most of these were nondescript. In the upper layer of area (b) a red-glazed fragment of the first century A.D. appeared. This, together with the fact that the upper layer continued unbroken over both inner and outer edges of the bedding and across the cutting for the border of the Roman orchestra, indicates that it was probably laid during the first Roman remodeling of the cavea when the blocks surrounding the Greek orchestra were removed. The lower layer of packing consisted of hard-packed earth and clay that almost entirely filled the bedding in the same way as the earth packing in the straight portion on the east side (area a). Evidently the bedding was cut to give a precise location for setting the blocks, and the packing was added to level out the natural grooves and irregularities in the hardpan as well as to compensate for the probably uneven bottom surfaces of the blocks themselves. The few sherds found at this level appear to be Hellenistic in date, although they are too small for precise identification.

10. The virgin clay is formed in layers that often slope downward, and a sandy stratum frequently appears below the top layer of greenish-white clay. Pockets of soft, sandy earth occur here and there as well as veins of almost rocklike hardness. This variation in consistency increased the difficulty of distinguishing between a cutting and a natural fault in the clay, and the present results are due to the keen eyes, skill, and great patience of our foreman, Dimitrios Papaioannou. In areas (b), (e), and (f) test trenches were opened to reveal the lower layer of hardpan below the clay orchestra bed; these reached to levels of −0.460 m, −0.553 m, and −0.452 m, respectively.

11. The edge in (b) is indistinct, but it is on the same general curve as the others.

Fig. 21. Edge of the second Greek orchestra at the center, looking northeast from the cavea. Two levels of packing are evident in the bedding for the pavement around the orchestra. The nail marks the Roman axis. Area (c) at right, (d) at left, Pl. III.

Fig. 22. Bedding for walk of second Greek period at the west end of area (c), Pl. III, looking south.

Fig. 23. Edge of orchestra at southwest side, looking south. Shows packing cleared to expose clay bed of orchestra; area (g) in foreground, area (f) at left background, Pl. III.

Farther on in area (f) and part of (g) it was impossible to distinguish an inner edge from the surrounding clay, inasmuch as the clay packing inside the bedding is often very similar to the clay bed of the orchestra, and the outer edge also disappears after area (e). The upper layer of packing, however, continued unbroken over the remainder of the border area (Figs. 1, 23). The inner edge can again be seen in area (g), but the line is not very distinct. At this point the cutting makes a right-angle turn to the outside (westward) and comes to an end after 1 m. The end line is in a position equivalent to the south edge of block G on the east side and may be taken as marking the westward extension of the curved portion of the orchestra.

Between the end of the curved portion and the annalemma (block E) no further bedding was discernible, and the area is covered with a clay layer at the same level as the other parts of the orchestra bed. We can only suppose that the western side of the orchestra was similar to the eastern one, terminating in a line perpendicular to the proskenion sill. An irregular cutting at the west side of this area might be the continuation of the earlier orchestra, although it is not precisely in the same line.

The analemmata and bedding for the stone border of the second Greek period were not located with reference to the axis of the Roman period (Pl. III), which was the same as that used for the skene and proskenion sill, but rather in relation to an axis 0.33 m to the east. This is determined from an extension of the south edge of block G and of the comparable cutting on the west side, which cross on a line bisecting the rectangular cutting at the south edge of the orchestra. Furthermore, it can be calculated that the curved section of the orchestra was drawn from a center on this axis, 0.33 m east of the Roman orchestra center and 6.90 m from the inner edge of the bedding (5.94 m south of the sill). Both inside and outside edges of the bedding, where they are preserved, fall on arcs of a circle with that center point, including the inner and outer ends at the east side where they begin to curve at block G.

On the west side the straight portion of the stone border, lying at right angles to the sill and reconstructed on the basis of the preserved east wing and with reference to the Greek axis (Pl. IV), falls 0.52 m inside the end of the analemma (E) and stops 0.42 m south of it. On the other side cutting F is unfortunately too large to furnish more detailed information about the exact position of the east analemma. It may be that the heavy stone border (0.54 m high and 0.65 m to 0.75 m wide) around the orchestra served also as a retaining wall for the earth that would have been added to support the first few rows of seats on the two wings since the virgin clay had been cut away for the cavea of the preceding period.[12] By moving the stone border out a little from the seats the walking area for the spectators was enlarged, and expense was kept to a minimum by leaving the inner section with a hard-packed earthen surface, perhaps covered with thin paving slabs. Thus, a walk about 1.22 m wide was provided, at least partially paved, a feature particularly desirable in wet weather.[13] The wide, shallow gutters at Epidauros, Eretria, and Oiniadai would have served a similar purpose since they were also used as walks by the audience.[14]

In the absence of further evidence (see n. 13, above), it must be concluded that the orchestra of this period was not equipped with a gutter, which is not unusual for a small theater (e.g., New Pleuron, Akrai, Thera, Apollo Erethimios near the city of Rhodes, Segesta, and Oropos). Perhaps the water found its way into an underground drain through an opening in the floor, although any evidence of such an arrangement vanished with the orchestra floor.[15] It is possible that the channel under the central passage

12. Although the edge of the first cavea is not preserved, it very likely followed the line indicated by the drainage channels (chap. 1, p. 15) but at a distance of at least 1 m outside the outer edge of the channels if manhole 1 were left free for drainage purposes (Pl. I).

13. It is just conceivable that the blocks of the stone border were cut to accommodate a very narrow (not over 0.45 m to 0.50 m wide), shallow (about 0.30 m) gutter at the edge of the orchestra, but no evidence of an outlet was found. For a discussion of the various forms and dimensions of theater gutters see O. Broneer, "The Ὄχετος in the Greek Theater," in *Classical Studies Presented to Edward Capps* (Princeton: Princeton University Press, 1936), pp. 29 ff. Another alternative for the function of the stone border is the foundation for a wooden proedria, but it was very narrow to support a series of seats.

14. The theater of Dionysos at Athens and the theaters at Delphi, Corinth, Piraeus, Priene, Syracuse, and Assos have broad walks lying between the gutter and the seats.

15. At Segesta and Oropos water from the orchestra found its way into the underground drain through a hole in the floor without the benefit of a gutter. The larger theater at Mantinea (orchestra radius 10.85 m) had no gutter or drain that has been found.

Fig. 24. Proskenion, looking west. Clay bank and scene-building at right.

of the skene, which received its present form in the first Roman period, existed in an earlier version in the same place. The short stretch of channel without stone sides just south of the proskenion sill and immediately beneath it could be a remnant of the original drain (chap. 3, p. 80).

In summary, the orchestra at this time had a total depth of 12.85 m, from the front of the proskenion sill to the inner edge of the stone border, and a width between the straight sides of 12.86 m. The architect apparently laid it out as a square. The radius of the curved section is 6.90 m, and the curve extends for only 140°. The long, straight sides and shallow curve of the center give the orchestra an arched-window shape that is unusually broad because the curve is less than the customary 180° or more.[16]

The location of the axis 0.33 m east of the center line of the proskenion, scene-building, and Roman orchestra is peculiar. The explanation may be simply inaccuracy on the part of the architect when he was laying out the new orchestra. Some evidence of attempts to compensate for the shift to the east is found in the longer ramp on the east side (11.65 m as opposed to 11.15 m on the west; below p. 52), and consequently a longer eastern parodos (12.20 m as opposed to 11.85 m on the west). Also, the eastern side of the skene is 0.23 m longer than the western.

The Skene

The scene-building at this time stood on the bank at the north edge of the orchestra in the same location and probably with the same general plan as the skene of the first theater. From the second phase, however, some of the foundations at orchestra level remain. On the west side the first course of the front wall is preserved (Fig. 24), and it continues along the west side of the central passage where two blocks of the second course and one from the third are standing (Pl. I, Fig. 25).

The first course consists of well-cut poros blocks measuring between 0.97 m and 1.35 m in length and between 0.40 m and 0.48 m in thickness; the course is 0.60 m high. The footing trench between the wall and the scarp behind is nearly equal to the thickness of the wall itself, and it is filled with red earth and poros chips that contained no pottery in the areas dug. The same fill at the top of the second course served as a bedding for the rubble masonry foundations that were placed behind the poros walls

Fig. 25. North end of central passage, looking west. Stairway of second Roman period at right.

16. See Pergamon where a shallow curve was necessary because of the precipitous terrain. The closest parallel to Isthmia is found in the theater at Xanthos, of which only an old sketch plan and description are available (F. Wieseler, *Theatergebäude und Denkmäler des Bühnenwesens bei den Griechen und Römern* [Göttingen: Vandenhoeck and Ruprecht, 1851]: Suppl. Pl. A, 4). There, too, straight sides were connected by a shallow curve in the center. The theater at Phlius, now under excavation, seems also to have had a very shallow curve, but without straight sides; see W. Biers, "Excavations at Phlius, 1970," *Hesperia* 40 (1971): 439–45, Fig. 8.

in the second Roman period. The workmanship on the poros blocks is good; the joints are tight and carefully fitted together without clamps. In the first course one edge of each joint and the bottom edges of the blocks are beveled.[17] In the front wall the beveling occurs on the east side of the joint, in the passage on the south side, so that construction apparently began at the south end of the passage and progressed both northward and westward from that point. From the placement of the pry holes, arranged singly or in groups of two or three on the blocks of the first course, we may conclude that the second course was begun at the north end of the passage and laid continuously to the west end of the skene. There is no doubt that the front wall and passage wall were laid at the same time.

The outer face of the front wall was smoothly finished to a line 0.23 m below the top of the first course (−0.04 m); below this line a rough surface projects unevenly about 0.02 m, and the beveled edge of the joints is more deeply cut (Fig. 9); this portion was certainly below the floor level inside the proskenion (see p. 53).

In the passage (Fig. 12) the finished edge is 0.02 m lower (−0.06 m) and the upper surface is finished smoothly with regular, slanting strokes of a flat chisel. Traces of anathyrosis appear on the badly worn ends of the second and third course blocks.

The second course of the passage wall (0.54 m high and preserved for a length of 1.85 m) consists of one block 1.35 m long and 0.51 m wide and part of another block that lies at right angles to the wall at the north end (Figs. 12, 26). The end block continues westward in what was probably the line of the rear wall of the skene, although no foundations or cuttings for them remain at this level (+0.74 m) or above it. The only foundation trench is that belonging to the Roman concrete wall that followed the same line. From the third course of the passage wall one block, 0.50 m high and broken at its west end, remains, turned slightly from its original position (Fig. 25).[18] It rests on the west half of the second course corner block; anathyrosis on the east face shows that it joined the northernmost block of the third course (Pl. I; the northeast corner of room III). The end of the passage wall seems simply to have turned the corner and abutted against a bank of earth; or, if there was a western continuation of the foundation, the Roman wall has obscured all trace of it.

On the east side of the passage all the blocks from the wall have been

Fig. 26. North end of the central passage, looking west. Roman extension of the passage at right.

17. Cf. the beveled edges and stone finishing technique on the foundations of the South Stoa at Corinth, built about 330 B.C. (O. Broneer, *The South Stoa and Its Roman Successors*, Vol. 1, pt. 4, of *Corinth*, pp. 20, 22, Pls. 1, 2, 4, 5) and the foundations for the front wall of the skene in the theater at Corinth, about 338–250 B.C. (Stillwell, *The Theatre*, pp. 35, 131, Fig. 24).

18. A setting line on the block beneath marks its original position and indicates that the third course had a thickness of 0.46 m.

removed. In the bottom of the foundation trench, 0.80 m wide, only a sinkage 0.40 m to 0.50 m wide is left to show the position of the wall. Single pry holes cut into the hardpan are still visible along its course. At the north end of the trench a deposit of reddish earth mixed with clay and poros chips filled the stair shaft of the first period (Fig. 10); the pottery included two fourth-century sherds and three from the third century. Thus, the shaft may have been used during the first part of the second period. The original clear width of the passage, 1.80 m, is marked by the western edge of the sinkage in the foundation trench.

In the front all the blocks have been removed on the east side, which was 6.88 m long or about 0.23 m longer than its western counterpart, perhaps due to the eastward shift in the axis of the orchestra. The east end of the wall would have joined the end wall of the proskenion where the northern-most block is cut with anathyrosis.

The floor level of the central passage at this time must have been approximately even with the lower edge of the finished surface on the west wall, about −0.06 m. A short flight of stairs at the north end of the passage probably led up to the area behind the skene. Trace of the first step can be detected on the west wall of the passage where the rough surface below floor level stops 0.36 m short of the north end of the passage (Fig. 26), and the wall is smoothly finished all the way down.

The ceiling of the passage may have been of wood, formed by the first floor of the skene. It could not have been higher than the skene floor, which in turn would have been level with the *logeion*, about +2.70 m (p. 55, Fig. 17). With an allowance of about 0.08 m for the thickness of the floor, a maximum height for the passage would have been about 2.62 m. It is also possible that the passage was vaulted like the one in the theater at Eretria,[19] although the over-all construction of the skene seems rather too modest to include a stone vault.

The upper part of the scene-building, which stood on top of the bank, has left no trace. Nevertheless, its existence is assured by the presence of the central passage and the proskenion that rose over 1 m above the bank and could hardly have stood by itself (Fig. 17).

The top of the bank as it now stands is of uneven height, varying between +1.18 m on the east and +2.13 m at the far west.[20] In the center its original level could never have been much over its present height of +1.34 m

19. See Fiechter, *Ant. Th.*, Vol. 8, Pl. 3. The vault had a height of 3.05 m and the passage was 2.05 m wide. With the same proportions a vault at Isthmia would have been about 2.70 m high on the outside, which is the approximate height of the proskenion as restored (below, p. 55).

20. The lowest sections are toward the center inside rooms III and IV. The east end of room V is +1.77 m, the west end +1.53 m; room IV is +1.18 m, room III +1.34 m, room II +1.56 m, and the west end of room I is +2.13 m.

because at the south edge of the cavea the hillside itself was only $+2.52$ m and a drop of at least 1 m in 25 m is to be expected for this slope. Although some reduction in the clay surface of the bank would not have been unusual in the course of the Roman reconstructions and the weathering of succeeding centuries, the absence of foundation cuttings for a stone skene in Greek times is probably not a consequence of later modifications. No stone structure appears to have been built at this time. Proof of this is supplied by the stretch of early, polygonal masonry (incorporated into the north wall of room IV; see Pl. I; Introduction, p. 6) that projects 0.16 m above the native clay, crossing the line of what would have been the rear wall of the skene at the north end of the central passage. Greek masons of the fourth century B.C. are not likely to have left such large rough stones in the footing trench of an ashlar wall.

The alternative is a skene built of wood, which is not without parallel even in the latter part of the fourth century B.C. On Delos building inscriptions from the last years of the century refer to a wooden skene that was not completely rebuilt in stone until the mid-third century.[21] The theater at Pergamon had a new, removable skene as late as the second century B.C. in order not to obstruct the narrow terrace on which it stood.[22] In the small deme theaters of Thorikos, Rhamnous, and Ikaria, the former probably dating from the end of the sixth century and the latter two from the fourth century, no remains of any scene-building have been identified, as is also the case at Morgantina. If one did exist, it would have been made of wood. In the theaters at Oropos and Sikyon, which also belong to the sunken orchestra class, and at Elis, Dodona, and Solunto in Sicily, post holes are preserved that seem to have held timbers for a wooden skene or *episkenion*,[23] in most cases later rebuilt in stone. A permanent stone building was apparently never provided for the small theater at Isthmia, which was used only biennially, and the destruction of Corinth in 146 B.C. put an end to further construction during the Greek epoch.

Vitruvius points out the advantages of wooden scene-buildings on ac-

21. J. Chamonard, "Théâtre de Délos," *BCH* 22 (1896): 279; Bulle, *Untersuchungen*, pp. 174 ff.; R. Vallois, *L'Architecture hellénique et hellénistique a Délos* (Paris: E. de Boccard, 1944), pp. 234–38.

22. Dörpfeld, *Gr. Th.*, p. 150, Fig. 61 (restored plan). See also W. Dörpfeld, "Die Arbeiten zu Pergamon 1904–05: Das griechische Theater der Akropolis," *AM* 32 (1907): 215 ff.

23. For Oropos see W. Dörpfeld, "Das Theater von Priene und die griechische Bühne," *AM* 49 (1924): 90–91. The principal discussion about Sikyon is in E. Fiechter, *Das Theater in Sikyon*, Vol. 3 of *Antike griechische Theaterbauten* (Stuttgart: W. Kohlhammer, 1931), pp. 10–12, Pl. 1. See idem, *Die baugeschichtliche Entwicklung des antikens Theaters* (Munich: O. Beck, 1914), pp. 34–36. The theater at Elis is currently being studied by V. Leon, but a final report has not been published; see O. Walter, "Vorläufiger Bericht über die Grabungen in Elis, 1914," *JOAI* 18 (1915): 68 ff. For Solunto see W. Fuchs and V. Tusa, "Archäologische Forschungen und Funde in Sizilien von 1955 bis 1964," *AA* (1964): 749–54.

coustical grounds because they furnished a sounding board for the performer's voice.[24] This was always an important factor in ancient theaters, which were open to the sky, and it would have been especially so at Isthmia where the theater seems to have been used primarily for musical and oratorical contests (see pp. 138, n. 1, 140, 142 ff.).

Beneath the floor of the skene there would have been an open space between 0.75 m and 1.50 m high, except for the area over the central passage. This space could have been used for storage, or it may simply have been filled in with earth.[25]

The over-all length of the scene-building was in all probability equal to the length of the proskenion, 15.60 m. The depth of the building, we may assume, corresponded to the length of the central passage, 6.03 m.[26]

The Proskenion

The proskenion was an important element in the theater at Isthmia both functionally and aesthetically. It provided a high platform particularly suited to single performers, and its multiple openings gave versatility of entrance and exit to those who performed in the orchestra.[27] In terms of design it formed a decorative screen concealing the retaining wall for the scarp and linking the sunken orchestra to the actual scene-building at the higher level. The bare retaining wall carried up as the front wall of the skene would have presented the audience with an uninspiring, two-story façade if there had been no other decoration than a single doorway at orchestra level.[28]

24. ". . . ab citharoedis qui, superiore tono cum volunt canere, avertunt se ad scaenae valvas et ita recipiunt ab earum auxilio consonantiam vocis" (Vitruvius, V. 5, 7). See Plutarch who recounts that when Alexander the Great requested a bronze proskenion for the theater at Pella the architect refused on the grounds that it would spoil the sound of the actors' voices ("χαλκοῦν Ἀλέξανδρον ἐν Πέλλῃ βουλόμενον ποιῆσαι τὸ προσκήνιον οὐκ εἴασεν ὁ τεχνίτης, ὡς διαφθεροῦντα τῶν ὑποκριτῶν τὴν φωνήν." *Moralia*, Disputio qua docetur ne suaviter . . ., 1096 b.)

25. At Corinth a similar space existed between the skene floor and the bedrock below; cf. Stillwell, *Theatre*, pp. 35–37, Pls. II, III, Figs. 26, 28, 29. The same arrangement is seen at Sikyon in the unexcavated portion of the first floor where a space of 0.50 m or more lay between the skene floor at +3.05 m and bedrock; see Fiechter, *Ant. Th.*, III, 21, Pl. I.

26. The later Greek scene-building at Corinth had nearly the same proportions (1:2.59), although the actual dimensions are greater (Stillwell, *Theatre*, pp. 33–35).

27. Cf. Dinsmoor, *AAG*, p. 300. He draws particular attention to this feature of the proskenion with reference to theaters with a sunken orchestra (Eretria, Corinth, Oropos, and Sikyon, to which we add Isthmia) because there was either no space at first floor level (as at Eretria and Isthmia) or only a limited area hollowed out of the bank.

28. The important point is that because a sunken orchestra necessitated a two-story scene-building, it would have required a different treatment than the simple one-story structure that the theater of Dionysos is supposed to have had in the fifth century B.C. (Cf. E. Fiechter, *Das Dionysos-Theater in Athen et al.,* Vol. 9 of *Antike griechische Theaterbauten* [Stuttgart: W. Kohlhammer, 1950]: 24–26, Fig. 7; Idem, *Ant. Th.*, 5: 16 ff.; 7: 68 ff., Figs. 30–34; T. B. L. Webster, "Staging and Scenery in the Ancient Greek Theatre," *Bulletin of the John*

Remains of the proskenion are more numerous than those of many other parts of the theater. The first course of both end walls, consisting of two blocks in each case, is complete and so is the entire stone sill. In the east end wall the northernmost block, 1.29 m by 0.51 m, is carefully finished in the same technique as the skene and passage walls. The heavy layer of mortar covering its northern end provided the bedding for the parodos wall of the second Roman period after the proskenion had been completely rebuilt (Figs. 11, 24). The next block to the south (marked D on Pl. I) is set at right angles to the first so that it extended eastward from the line of the wall (see Pl. VI). Its (east-west) length is 1.08 m and its width 0.47 m; the top of the east end has been cut and also worn down about 0.08 m from its original surface, probably in the second Roman period when there was an entrance to the proskenion there. Block D served as a corner member, bonded into both the proskenion wall and the retaining wall for the north side of the parodos (Pls. VI, VII). The top surface of the east end slants upward (Fig. 11, Pl. VI) following the slope of the parodos; later, when the proskenion wall had been dismantled, the sloping surface was cut down another few centimeters at its west end and the surface made level for the Roman entrance. (The notch in the block to the north was cut at the same time.)[29]

The same arrangement is seen at the west end of the proskenion (Pl. V). The northernmost block is 1.35 m by 0.48 m; the second block (marked C on Pl. I) is comparable to D in position and function, although it differs in some details, to be described below. Marks left from the second course show that it was 0.435 m thick. The inside face of the wall was smoothly finished in the same manner as the retaining wall at the back of the proskenion (i.e., the front wall of the skene), and beneath the smooth surface exposed to view the rough lower portion projects slightly. On the basis of workmanship and the manner in which the end wall joins the retaining wall, we can assume that the proskenion and the skene are contemporary.

On block C the top surface of the west half slopes upward in the same manner as D, and there are the same signs of wear and the same small notch in the next block to the north. The only difference is that the recutting of the sloping surface does not seem to have been finished, and the

---

Rylands Library 42 [1960]: 500–6; Dinsmoor, "The Athenian Theater of the Fifth Century," *Studies* 1: 322 ff). Thus, it is not surprising to find a shallow porch across the first floor even in the earliest skene (chap. 1, p. 20) and a fully developed proskenion in the second. A similar sequence may have taken place at Sikyon, Oropos, and Eretria where a poros sill underlies the marble one in each case.

29. Marks on the sloping surface indicate its original terminus before recutting. The section toward the west end shows none of the wear evident on the higher portion of the east end, and it is apparent that an extra member was inserted to level off the block when it became the threshold for an entrance to the Roman proskenion.

surface was probably leveled off with packed earth rather than by means of an added piece of stone (see n. 29).

Two blocks from the corner between the west wall of the proskenion and the retaining wall along the north side of the west parodos were found to have been reused in a rectangular base of the second Roman period. The base stood in the northwest corner of the proskenion (Fig. 27, Pl. V; block A inset). The largest of the blocks (A), which seems to be complete, is 1.05 m long by 0.495 m wide (maximum) at what would have been its east end when it was in place (Fig. 27).[30] It is now about 0.25 m high, perhaps less than the original height, due to wear. A long section of one face is cut back at an 8° angle to the remainder of the face; the slanted portion is covered with a layer of Roman stucco applied at a period of refurbishing to conceal the heavily weathered surface of the soft stone. Of the second block (B) (Fig. 27), only half remains, both of length and height. A short section of the slanting face is preserved, with the same angle in relation to the rest of the face as on block A. The rectangular end of these blocks is the right size to have joined the end wall of the proskenion, and the slanted section would have formed part of the parodos wall (Pl. V). Thus, the blocks tell us that the interior angle between the parodos wall and the proskenion was 172°. On both blocks, the section that joined the proskenion has been roughly hacked off on its outer face for a space of 0.42 m, and it is this portion that would have formed the south end of the

30. The block tapers to 0.385 m at what would have been its west end.

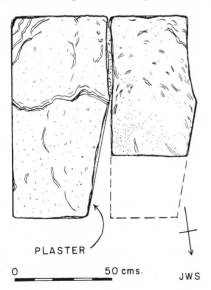

Fig. 27. Blocks A and B built into the northwest corner of the proskenion, seen from above, looking south. West end wall of the proskenion at right.

PLASTER

0   50 cms.

JWS

1969

Pl. VII. East end of the proskenion, conjectural
isometric reconstruction.

proskenion end wall. On the back of both blocks there are cuttings for anathyrosis where they would have joined the next blocks in the end wall.

On blocks C and D peculiar recesses are cut 0.05 m deep into their south faces. These cuttings are clearly visible in Figs. 28 and 29 and in isometric drawings of the east and west ends of the sill (Pls. V, VI). The south face of D is smoothly cut back over most of its surface, with the exception of two bands, one about 0.13 m wide along the east edge, the other 0.07 m to 0.10 m wide along the top, now largely broken away. The present stone sill stops 0.21 m short of the east end of the recess, and the top surface of the sill lies 0.07 m below its top. A thin, vertical flange of stone (0.05 m wide and 0.07 m high) has been left along the inner edge of the sill where it fitted under the top of the recess.

Block C on the west side has a similarly indented surface with a projecting band left at the top and west end. Here, however, the end band and the eastern part of the top have been cut away, leaving the top band intact only where it was protected by the parodos wall (Pl. V). Instead of the vertical flange found on the east end of the sill, a groove 0.055 m wide was

Fig. 28. East end of the proskenion sill where it meets block D (Pl. VI), looking north.

Fig. 29. West end of the proskenion sill where it meets block C (Pl. V), looking northeast.

cut in the top of the sill block so that it could be slipped into the recess. The rough faces of the two corner blocks A and B show that a few centimeters of the south face of the proskenion end wall were chiseled from its original surface that included the top band on block C. This may have facilitated the insertion of the sill block, and was probably done at the same time.

The differences in treatment between the east and west ends of the sill are very likely due to circumstances encountered during construction. It may have been that the west end was laid first and adjustments made by cutting a sloping groove into the top of the sill block, and then sliding the sill block into place. Perhaps when the builders reached the east end they found that the surface of the sill was 0.07 m lower than the top of the recess in D, so after they set the sill block into the recess they cut down its top surface to the level of the rest of the sill. This left the projecting flange at the rear edge of the block (Pl. VI). We do not know if the proskenion end wall was modified at the east end.

Such a difficult arrangement at both ends of the sill could hardly have been planned in relation to the present stone sill; a change in construction and probably a lapse of time are indicated. This is also evident from the inner corners of blocks C and D, which were crudely cut back to receive the blocks of the present sill. The irregularity of the workmanship is such that the stone sill does not appear to have been part of the original proskenion.

The recesses on blocks C and D must then be referred to an earlier sill, which fitted into them. Further evidence for the presence of this sill is furnished by a cutting in clay (only about 0.30 m wide) at each end of the present sill (Fig. 28, Pl. VI. The cutting does not appear on Pl. V, showing the west end of the sill, but it is similar to the one on the east side). If we measure from the outer edge of the recesses, the earlier sill would have been about 0.32 m longer than the present one. On the basis of the cutting at the ends, it was also 0.20 m narrower. Then what was the function of the recesses? They can have served no useful purpose for a stone sill, but if the sill was made of wood, the overlap at the top of the joint would have prevented moisture from collecting between the end wall and the sill.[31] No other information can be ascertained about the proskenion façade of this

---

31. Although it may seem strange to suggest a proskenion sill of wood resting in the ground, wooden piles are recommended for stylobate foundations where the soil is soft (Vitruvius, III. 4, 2) and for the substructure of brick or stone flooring even when laid upon open ground (VII. 1, 5). Cf. Theophrastus, Περὶ φυτῶν ἱστορίας, V. 7, 5; 4, 3; 7, 6. The foundations of the Temple of Athena at Troy were reinforced by a filling of sand supported by wooden posts about 0.15 m in diameter (W. Dörpfeld, *Troja und Ilion* [Athens: Beck and Barth, 1902], 1: 217 f., 220). See R. Martin, *Matériaux et Techniques*. Part I of *Manuel d'Architecture Grecque* (Paris: A. et J. Picard, 1965), pp. 14–15.

period, although it probably differed little from the one that followed it.

One other feature should be noted in the placement of the sill. It lay across the end walls of the proskenion instead of being inserted between them as was the case in many other theaters (e.g., Oropos, Eretria, Syracuse, Segesta, Priene, Megalopolis, Akrai, and New Pleuron). Only the theaters at nearby Corinth and Sikyon (first period with poros sill) and perhaps at Thera had a similar arrangement.

The Ramps and Parodoi

Two parodoi entered the orchestra, swept back at an angle of 8° from the front line of the proskenion (above, p. 47). Due to the low level of the orchestra, the parodoi had a steep incline, and a long retaining wall was erected along the clay scarp at the north side of each parodos. Blocks A, B, and C were bonded into this wall on the west side and block D on the east. The first course was evidently laid with the blocks following the incline, as the sloping sections on C and D indicate. The second and upper courses would presumably have followed suit until the top, where the final course would have been wedge-shaped with the bottom sloping and the top almost horizontal (Pl. VII).[32] The walls were removed in the second Roman period.

Along the north side of the parodoi ramps very likely led to the top of the proskenion.[33] Where the native clay of the bank was lower than the top of the proskenion earth would have been brought in to raise the floor of the ramp, and the parodos wall would have acted as a retaining wall for the ramp. The fact that the parodoi walls were bonded into the end walls of the proskenion (see blocks A and B) indicates that they were part of the same construction that would also have included the ramps.

The length of the ramps cannot be restored with certainty, but some indication of their extent may be provided by the analemmata of the first Roman period, which were erected while the retaining walls for the ramps were still standing. In view of the fact that Roman analemmata are usually parallel to the skene, their more pronounced angle here could have resulted from a desire to follow approximately the line of the earlier retaining walls along the opposite side of the parodoi (chap. 3, p. 63). Thus, on the west side the bend in the analemma, which corresponds to no apparent feature of the cavea, may instead have been related to the west end of the ramp wall (Pl. I). The eastern end of the east analemma, which had no upper

32. At Corinth the first course sloped up, but the rest were horizontal; Stillwell, *Theatre*, Fig. 32; Pl. V c, and p. 39. In most instances the entire coursing of the parodoi walls is horizontal; e.g., at Eretria and Oropos.

33. Ramps are usually found in theaters where the skene and proskenion are approximately the same length; e.g., Eretria, Sikyon, Oropos, Corinth, Elis, and Epidauros.

extension, can be considered to have corresponded to the upper end of the ramp wall on that side. If this correspondence is true, then the ramp on the west would have been about 11.15 m long and that on the east 11.65 m, as shown on the restored plan (Pl. IV).

Along the top of what is now the south edge of the clay bank there is a footing trench for an ashlar wall on the east and west sides where later rooms I, II, and V of the Roman skene were built. In the second Greek period these small walls would have supported the rear (north) sides of the ramps where the earth fill necessary to raise the ramp floor to the height of the proskenion would have been higher than the clay bank.[34] The trench is best preserved on the west side where it runs for 8.40 m, from the west end to within 2.27 m of the skene (Fig. 1).[35] The cutting varies in width between 0.65 m and 0.75 m and in depth between 0.30 m at the east end and about 1.00 m at the west. The clay bank slopes down to the east, and the floor of the cutting is horizontal. At the time of excavation the eastern section was entirely filled with chunks of clay packed so firmly that they were almost indistinguishable from the natural clay. No pottery was found in the fill. One rectangular limestone block, badly weathered, remains *in situ* at the west end (1.16 m by 0.42 m and 0.57 m high). Perhaps two or three blocks to the east of it also remained in place when the supporting wall for the Roman parodos vault was built, because some trace of them is visible in the mortar of the Roman wall. A similar foundation trench exists on the east side of the skene, but all blocks have been removed and the cutting was completely filled with hard-packed clay containing a few sherds of early Roman date. These retaining walls appear to have been removed when the skene was enlarged in the first Roman period (chap. 3, pp. 74–75).

The floors of the parodoi were originally higher than they are at present (perhaps 0.50 m or more), because the foundation trenches for the north walls are merely shallow cuttings at the lower ends and can be traced for a distance of only about 3.50 m. On the south side, also, the first course of the analemma would have lain below the parodos floor.

The ends of the analemmata (block E and cutting F) would have marked the lower ends of the parodoi, and they are approximately in line with the ends of the proskenion. The parodoi would thus have had a clear width of

34. At Sikyon a wall about 0.82 m thick stood at the back of the proskenion ramps and served to separate them from the skene ramps behind (Fiechter, *Ant. Th.* 3: 19–21, Fig. 2, Pls. 1, 5). Both at Sikyon and Isthmia such a wall would also have been useful to conceal entrances at the side of the skene. Walls of this kind are found too at Epidauros (A. von Gerkan and W. Müller-Wiener, *Das Theater von Epidauros* [Stuttgart: W. Kohlhammer, 1961], p. 61, Pl. 12) and are restored by Fiechter at Oropos, but without any apparent evidence (Fiechter, *Ant. Th.* 1, Pl. 8).

35. This gap of 2.27 m is probably due to a step up in the coursing to follow the rise of the ramp floor.

about 3.00 m at the outside (upper) end, and they would have widened to about 3.50 m at the edge of the orchestra. On the assumption that the bend in the west analemma (and the upper end of the east one) of the Roman period may indicate the upper ends of the Greek analemmata as well as the beginning of the ramps, the total length of the west parodos would have been about 11.85 m and the east parodos 12.20 m.[36]

The Proskenion of the Third Greek Period

The third Greek period is distinguished only by the insertion of a new proskenion sill and the proskenion façade that it supported; the end walls remained unchanged, and the rest of the theater seems to have continued without alteration.

The proskenion façade on the stone sill stretched for 16.00 m (including end walls) across the front of the skene, and its roof formed a *logeion* 2.34 m wide, accessible from the scene-building and from the ramps at the ends. Fortunately, the entire sill is preserved with cuttings, incised lines, and worn places on its surface from which the position of the supports and the other essential features of the proskenion can be reconstructed (see Pl. VII).

The sill is composed of well-cut, soft limestone blocks 0.62 m high and varying between 1.23 m and 1.43 m in length and between 0.56 m and 0.65 m in width. The front has a drafted edge about 0.04 m high to provide a finished surface toward the orchestra (Pl. VI).[37] Below the drafting the blocks are roughly finished and were obviously below ground level. The tightly fitting, beveled joints resemble those of the skene, and the backs of the blocks are finished in like fashion with regular, slanting strokes of a flat chisel. The blocks project unevenly at the back, inside the proskenion, which indicates that the floor would have been at the same level as the sill. A mason's mark in the form of the letter K appears on the rear face of the fourth block from the east end. The numerous grooves and cuttings and irregularly spaced, deeply cut, shifting notches that mark the surface of the sill do not seem to be related to the use of the sill at this time (chap. 4, pp. 105–6).

The position of the proskenion supports on the sill is shown by a series of small rectangular cuttings (0.105 m to 0.13 m long, 0.07 m to 0.075 m wide, and about 0.03 m deep) that occur at intervals of 1.27 m to 1.37 m (Fig. 24). That the supports stood at one side of each of these cuttings is indicated by the setting lines used to center the westernmost of them

36. They are so restored on Pl. IV. The longer parodos and ramp on the east side probably was planned to compensate for the eastward shift of the orchestra axis; above, pp. 38–39.

37. Similar draftings are found on the poros and marble sills at Eretria; on the poros sill it is 0.11 m high, on the marble one 0.08 m high (Fiechter, *Ant. Th.* 8, Pls. 3, 4; on pp. 24–25 the figures have been reversed, but I take the drawings as more reliable).

(Pl. V) and the second one from the east end (Pl. VI, Fig. 30). On the west half of the sill the cuttings were on the east side of the supports; the reverse was true on the east half. The center opening had a cutting on both sides. If there were setting lines for the other supports, they have since disappeared.

The width of the supports may be calculated in the following manner: the centering line for the second support from the east end is located 0.15 m from the west end of a low projection or curb on the sill (Pl. VI, Fig. 30).[38] On the other side the line is only 0.13 m from the edge of the

Fig. 30. Close-up of proskenion sill, looking south. At left is raised curb. Between curb and rectangular cutting at right is the setting line for the second pier from the east end (arrows).

38. The curb is broken off at its east end, but it was originally 0.985 m long, 0.115 m wide, and 0.035 m high. Faint traces of other curbs are discernible along the sill, although they were completely chiseled off in Roman times and the surface of the sill is too damaged for exact measurements.

rectangular cutting. Since the support could have overlapped the cutting but would have had to fit tightly against the curb, the space of 0.15 m may be taken as half the width of the support and the total width would have been 0.30 m. Further confirmation of this is given by a worn place on the stone that shows where the support overlapped the rectangular cutting by 0.02 m (Pl. VI). A comparable worn place was found on the north side of the final rectangular cutting on the east end, so that the overlapping was evidently an intentional part of the design. A setting line for the front of the two easternmost supports appears 0.05 m from the edge of the sill (Pl. VI), which gives the amount of setback for the series. The thickness of the supports is revealed by a cutting for the back of the final support on the east, 0.47 m from the setting line for the front. Therefore, the proskenion façade consisted of twelve supports, 0.30 m wide and 0.47 m thick, recessed 0.05 m from the front of the sill and with intervals of 1.04 m to 1.07 m between them.[39] At the ends the openings diminished to 0.97 m on the west and 0.985 m on the east.[40]

It is impossible to determine the actual height of the proskenion from the evidence we have. On analogy with other theaters, a proskenion with twelve supports and a length of 15.17 m would have been about 2.70 m high including the entablature (Pl. VII, Fig. 17).[41] The absence of any marks on the sill where the supports rested, of the kind that are visible at Epidauros and on the later sills at Oropos and Sikyon and on numerous others, is a good sign that the twelve supports were made of wood, probably rectangular in section.[42] The entire scheme appears to have been a

39. The interaxial spacing, exclusive of the openings at both ends, was 1.34 m to 1.37 m, close to that found at Oropos, which was 1.355 m to 1.360 m, and at Thasos, which was 1.36 m to 1.37 m (F. Salviat, "Le Bâtiment de Scène du Théâtre de Thasos," *BCH* 84 [1960]: 309).

40. Smaller openings at the ends of the proskenion are also seen at Oropos, where they diminish from about 1.09 m to 1.065 m, and at Priene, where they go from 1.50 m to 1.40 m (A. von Gerkan, *Das Theater von Priene* [Munich-Berlin: F. Schmidt, 1921], Pl. XXV). In both cases, as at Isthmia, the center opening was not increased.

41. The theater at Priene had a proskenion of twelve piers and a total height of 2.72 m on a sill 21.23 m long (von Gerkan, *Priene*, pp. 39-45, Fig. 4). At Oropos the proskenion of ten supports was 2.49 m high on a sill 12.36 m long (Fiechter, *Ant. Th.* 1: 15-16, Pl. 4). The larger theater at Eretria had a proskenion of fourteen supports and a total height of 3.30 m on a sill 19.85 m long. A lower proskenion of about 2.76 m is estimated for the theater at Corinth from the slope of the ramps, although the long sill (about 22.30 m) would have accommodated fourteen supports (Stillwell, *Theatre*, p. 39, Pl. III). The ratio of the total height of these proskenia to the length of the sill varies: Oropos 1:5, Eretria 1:6, Priene 1:8, Corinth 1:8; but the relative height appears to decrease as the length increases. For Isthmia, with a sill of 15.17 m between the end piers and with twelve uniform supports placed relatively close together, a height of about 2.70 m seems appropriate. Its ratio would then be 1:5.5, which would place it between Oropos and Eretria. See Bulle, *Untersuchungen*, p. 299, and Rizzo, *Il Teatro greco di Siracusa*, p. 90, for lists of proskenia and their dimensions.

42. The earliest proskenia of which there is record seem to have been made of wood. In the beginning perhaps only a simple skeleton of wooden posts and architrave was set up in front

simple one without the ornamentation common to later stone proskenia.[43]

At either end of the sill stood a pier larger than the other supports (Pls. V, VI, VII), 0.43 m wide on the east and 0.40 m on the west and projecting 0.08 m from the line of the other supports. In addition to these distinctions, the end supports may well have been made of stone, continued to the top of the architrave. Perhaps due to the fact that this is not the original sill and façade, the final piers do not correspond to the end walls of the

of the scene-building, as is suggested by the often-quoted anecdote about the courtesan Nannion of the fourth century B.C. Athenaeus records: "'Ἀντιφάνης δὲ ἐν τῷ περὶ Ἑταιρῶν 'Προσκήνιον' φησίν 'ἐπεκαλεῖτο ἡ Νάννιον, ὅτι πρόσωπον τε ἀστεῖον εἶχε καὶ ἐχρῆτο χρυσίοις καὶ ἱματίοις πολυτελέσι, ἐκδῦσα δὲ ἦν αἰσχροτάτη'." (Athenaeus, xiii, 587, b 2; cf. A. Pickard-Cambridge, *The Theatre of Dionysos in Athens* [Oxford: Clarendon Press, 1946], pp. 157-58; Dinsmoor, *AAG*, pp. 298 ff.). According to Pickard-Cambridge, this reveals that the proskenion was "something decorative concealing something plain," while Dinsmoor adds that it "could easily be slipped away, leaving only bald nakedness." Both equate the proskenion with the clothes Nannion wore, which leaves Nannion herself as equivalent to the bare skene. On the other hand, if the anecdote is read literally, it is the complete Nannion who is called proskenion; when dressed she resembles the proskenion decorated for a performance (with *pinakes*, draperies, garlands, etc.), but without these trappings both she (mere skin and bones?) and the bare framework of the proskenion are most ugly to behold. There seems to be no indication about the permanence of the structure or its magnitude; a series of wooden posts and architrave would satisfy the condition of bare ugliness. At Delos an inscription from 305 B.C. (*IG* XI. 2. 142, line 43) records the purchase of τὰ περὶ τὴν σκηνὴν . . . ξύλα for over 551 drachmai and χαλχῶν πρὸς τοὺς πίνακας (1. 48). Another inscription (*IG*, XI. 2. 153, line 194) mentions the payment of 410 drachmai . . . τοῖς τὴν σκηνὴν ἐργολαβήσασι καὶ τὸ προσκήνιον. Bulle (*Untersuchungen*, p. 180) assigns the latter to the same period as number 142, about 300 B.C. The ambiguity of such building inscriptions and their use of terminology prohibits any definite conclusions (see Pickard-Cambridge, *Theatre of Dionysos*, p. 207); nevertheless, an expenditure of over 551 drachmai for "wood [placed] around the skene" seems to suggest that the wood was intended for some major construction such as a substantial proskenion to which the *pinakes*, mentioned five lines later, belonged. Vallois, however (*Architecture hellénique*, p. 236, n. 1), relates number 142 only to the skene construction and assigns the first proskenion colonnade of wood to about 282 B.C. when a building inscription again mentions *pinakes* and proskenion (*IG*, XI, 2, 158 A, lines 67-69). At Eretria, Sikyon, and Oropos a poros sill is found under the later marble sill, and it is probable that in each case it carried wooden supports, although considerable discussion has centered on this question, which is related to the date for the introduction of the proskenion. Bieber (*Greek and Roman Theater*, pp. 109 ff.) includes a full discussion of the theories. For Eretria see Fiechter (*Ant. Th.* 8: 24, Fig. 32), who rejects a proskenion on the sill, and Dinsmoor (*AAG*, p. 300, n. 1), who affirms the wooden proskenion but not until the middle of the third century B.C., to which K. Schefold agrees on historical grounds ("Die Grabungen in Eretria im Herbst 1964 und 1965: Das Theater," *Antike Kunst* 9 [1966]: 110-12) and discusses the various reconstructions and dating of the theater. For Sikyon see Dinsmoor, *AAG*, p. 299, n. 6; Fiechter (*Ant. Th.* 3: 29, Figs. 19-20) and Bulle (*Untersuchungen*, pp. 195 ff.) assign a poros capital to the poros sill, but it was not found in the theater and is not necessarily connected with it. At Oropos, Dörpfeld (*Gr. Th.*, p. 102) believed that there was an original wooden proskenion, but he gives no more specific evidence than the poros sill.

43. A survey of proskenion supports is given in Dinsmoor, *AAG*, pp. 299-302, Bulle, *Untersuchungen*, pp. 297 ff., and Pickard-Cambridge, *Theatre of Dionysos*, p. 217. Indications for simple rectangular piers (probably wooden), such as those proposed for Isthmia, are found at Orchomenos in Arcadia and at Mantinea.

proskenion, which, on the west at least, may have been chiseled down especially to receive it. It is unusual to have a larger support at the end of the colonnade, because the end walls themselves customarily extended to the front of the sill and the sill was inserted between them. Here the stone supports took their place and would have appeared as *antae* serving to frame the wooden portion of the façade.

For a small theater used only for a few days every two years, a removable proskenion would have been a practical arrangement. The supports, architrave, and *logeion* floor, all made of wood, could have been easily assembled and then taken down and stored under cover until the next festival. In this way they would have served for a long time with a minimum of upkeep.

At the time of the performances the intervals between the supports would have been closed by wooden panels or *pinakes* bearing painted decoration (Pl. VII). These were commonly used in all proskenia,[44] but at Isthmia the method of attaching them is almost unique. The small rectangular depressions at one side of each opening evidently contained plates with sockets into which pivots were fitted so that the panels could swing open and closed. This is the most probable explanation for the cuttings inasmuch as they are too small to have held wooden posts.[45] Furthermore, one other apparently similar arrangement has been found on Rhodes.[46] The plate would have been held in place by the piers that overlapped the cuttings by about 0.02 m according to the marks on the sill. A pivot on the corresponding top corner of the *pinax* would have been inserted into an appropriate hole in the architrave.[47] The panel would thus have operated like a swinging door, and the free side would have been fastened by a bolt to the adjoining pier.[48] The existence of a rectangular cutting at either side of the center opening points to a double center door as at Oropos, New Pleuron, and Epidauros.[49] The drawing (Pl. VII) shows

44. Cf. Dinsmoor, *AAG*, p. 303.

45. At Sikyon, on the other hand, where the holes are larger and deeper and occur at both sides of the openings, the suggestion of wooden posts for the fastening of *pinakes* seems most reasonable, Fiechter, *Ant. Th.* 3: 13–14, Figs. 6, 7, 9. Cf. Bulle, *Untersuchungen*, pp. 195 ff.

46. The small theater next to the temple of Apollo Erethimios near the city of Rhodes was almost completely demolished during the Second World War in order to build a pillbox at the top of the cavea. According to the excavation report, small blocks of marble were found inserted into rectangular holes in the sill and each carried a small round depression in the center (G. Jacopi, "Il Tempio e il Teatro di Apollo Eretimio," *Clara Rhodos* 2 [1932]: 114–16, Figs. 34–35). The interaxial spacing was about 1 m, but no other measurements are given.

47. For the center door at Oropos two such holes can be seen cut into the architrave, and two corresponding pivot holes were cut in the sill (Fiechter, *Ant. Th.* 1: 15–16, Figs. 2, 4 [block PA 5]).

48. See the slots cut into the sides of the proskenion supports at Oropos, Priene, and Thasos.

49. The cutting on the east side of the opening was very nearly obliterated by a later water channel, but its east edge is discernible.

Fig. 31. East end wall of the proskenion and sill,
looking south. Arrow marks the cutting in the end
wall to accommodate the *pinax* as it swung inward.

how the proskenion may have appeared at this time; the appearance of a sloping floor is a result of the isometric projection, for of course the proskenion floor would have been level.

That at least one of the *pinakes* actually did swing on its pivot is revealed by a cutting on the inner face of the east end wall of the proskenion. The stone has been cut back about 0.02 m, beginning at the junction between the wall and the sill (Fig. 31). The cutting ends at a point 0.94 m from the center of the rectangular sinkage for the first pivot, a distance precisely equal to the opening between the proskenion supports and thus equal to the width of the first *pinax* (Pls. VI, VII). Clearly, the end wall had prevented the panel from opening fully, and a remedy was found in chiseling off just enough of the inner face to allow the *pinax* to lie flat against it.

The low projection or curb across the first opening at the east end of the sill would have helped to hold the *pinax* in place when the panel closed against it from behind, in the manner of a door against a threshold. Although the sill retains little of its original surface, faint traces of similar projections are discernible in a few places. Nothing precisely like this is found in other theaters. At Oropos, Oiniadai, and Thasos the sill itself is cut down at the rear of each intercolumniation so that the *pinax*, slipped in from the back, was braced against the higher section in front.[50] This device seems to be an improvement over the curb-like projection at Isthmia and evidently reflects a later development inasmuch as the proskenia mentioned above are fifty to a hundred years later than the Isthmian one.[51]

In summary, the scene-building at this period was a rectangular structure of wood about 15.60 m long and 6.03 m deep (Pls. I, IV, Fig. 17). Because of the sunken orchestra floor, the rooms of the skene were located at the second-story level, and there was no open space below them except a central passage, 1.80 m wide, connecting the proskenion with the rear of the skene. The proskenion, 2.34 m deep, extended for 16.00 m across the front of the bank, making a smooth transition between the low orchestra and the skene above. The room(s) of the skene opened onto the roof of the proskenion *(logeion)*, which would have been approximately 2.70 m above the orchestra, and was probably used by the poets, musicians, and orators who competed at the Isthmian festival. They entered the *logeion* either from the skene or by means of the ramps at both ends of the proskenion.

50. Fiechter, *Ant. Th.* 1, Pl. 3, Fig. 4–5; 2, Pls. 1, 3, 4; Salviat, *BCH* 84 (1960), Fig. 6.
51. The marble proskenion at Oropos is dated by its inscription to about 200 B.C. (Dörpfeld, *Gr. Th.*, pp. 100–101; Fiechter, *Ant. Th.* 1: 27); Oiniadai received a proskenion probably toward the end of the third century B.C. when the seats were inscribed (B. Powell, "Oeniadae: The Theater," *AJA* 8 [1904]: 183). The marble proskenion at Thasos is placed in the early part of the third century B.C. on the basis of its inscription and its resemblance to other buildings of that period (Salviat, *BCH* 84 [1960]: 308, 313).

General Chronology of the Second and Third Greek Periods

It has been shown above (chap. 1, pp. 24–26) that manholes 1 and 2 of the underground drain were filled up and the drain abandoned in the second half of the fourth century B.C. This would have been the logical time in the history of the sanctuary for the remodeling of the theater, and the few Hellenistic sherds in the packing inside the bedding at the edge of the orchestra point to a date near the end of the fourth century.

Further, a date *post quem* for the proskenion is provided by a silver coin of Alexander, minted at Abydos in Asia Minor in 324 B.C. (IC 349, Fig. 32).[52] The coin was found about 0.28 m south of the sill and about the same distance east of the center axis, only a few centimeters above hard-pan. This is approximately 0.40 m below the orchestra floor; the coin was very likely dropped when a foundation trench was opened for the sill (though we cannot be certain whether it was the first or second one). Another coin (IC 739, a bronze from Hermione, 350–322 B.C.) came to light 0.31 m south of the west end of the sill and level with its surface. Although the coin was not in a closed context, its close proximity to the sill and its fourth-century date warrant mention of it in connection with the chronology.

The date of the second Greek phase of the theater, then, would fall near the end of the fourth century B.C., and the substitution of a stone sill would have followed soon after. This was the last apparent alteration to the theater until mid-first century A.D. Although it may have undergone some changes and repairs during the next century and a half, until the destruction of Corinth in 146 B.C., the plan evidently remained the same. Beyond that, its poor state of preservation does not permit any further speculation.

52. The late Eunice Work kindly gave me this information; it will be included in her work on the silver coins of the Greek period from Isthmia. See Broneer, *Klio* 39 (1961): 266. The obverse exhibits the head of Alexander the Great, the reverse a statue of Olympian Zeus. The coin could not have been long in circulation since it shows only moderate signs of wear.

Fig. 32. Silver coin of Alexander the Great (IC 349).

3

The First Roman Period

Repairs and alterations at Isthmia were finally undertaken a century after control of the sanctuary had passed to the Roman colony at Corinth. Rebuilding operations in the theater preceded a visit from the emperor Nero who personally competed in the games and musical contests. At this time the retaining walls along the north side of the parodoi received a fresh coat of plaster and long wings were added to the scene-building, which itself must have been built anew. The fine analemmata of the new cavea begun at this time are still preserved to a height of one and two courses. In the northeast area a new building was constructed, but the full development of this section as part of the theater complex did not come until the second Roman rebuilding.

The Cavea

A major undertaking in this period was the remodeling and enlargement of the cavea, which included new beddings for the seat blocks and new analemmata. The new upper section, which would have greatly increased the seating capacity, seems never to have progressed beyond the initial stages. Only the west analamma was completed to its full length; its eastern counterpart stops at the top of the parodos (Figs. 33, 34).

The west analemma was laid out in two sections. The first one extended for 9.50 m, from the orchestra to what was probably the western end of the parodos where the retaining wall from the preceding period remained standing along the north side.[1] At that point the analemma bends slightly to the south and continues westward for another 13.25 m. This represents the intended addition to the auditorium (Pl. I). A bend in the analemma is unusual, but it removed seats from the outer edge of the cavea where the visibility would have been poor.[2] In the lower section the orientation of the wall differs little from that of its Greek predecessor, which is very likely due to the presence of the retaining wall of the parodos opposite it (Fig. 18). Thus the direction and appearance of the parodos would have remained essentially the same as in the earlier period.[3]

1. The heavy coat of plaster with a lime mortar base on the outside face of block A that was applied in order to cover a deeply weathered surface is a clear indication that the parodos wall was standing at the time of the first Roman remodeling (see chap. 2, p. 47).

2. Cf. the theater at Hephaistia where the bend in the analemma of the Greek period is similar though more acute (G. Libertini, "Scavi a Lemno," *Annuario della Regia Scuola Archeologica di Atene*, N. S. 1–2 [1939–40]: 221–23, Fig. 2). The same effect is gained at Epidauros by setting the upper extension of the analemmata back one-half the width of the end *kerkides* (Von Gerkan, *Epidauros*, Pl. II).

3. This is one of the unusual characteristics of the first Roman period at Isthmia, which show that the theater, though substantially rebuilt, retained its Greek plan. In purely Roman theaters (e.g., the odeum at Corinth, theater of Marcellus at Roma, odeum at Pompeii, and theater at Ostia) and Greek theaters remodeled on Roman lines (e.g., theaters at Corinth, Sparta, Pompeii, Syracuse, and Segesta), the analemmata were placed parallel to the scene-building. In some Greek theaters the slanting analemmata were left unchanged in Roman

Fig. 33. West end of the west parodos, looking south. Ashlar analemma of first Roman period behind heavier wall of second Roman period.

Fig. 34. West parodos, looking east from the west end of analemma.

This Greek feature and others noted below may be in part the result of economy in incorporating as much of the older building as possible and replacing only what was necessary. It is difficult for us to ascertain the condition of the theater at the time of the rebuilding in the first century A.D. The system of retaining walls along the clay scarp, both inside the proskenion and central passage and along the parodoi, certainly remained standing, and they would have influenced the design of the cavea adjacent to the parodoi and the general outline of the skene (see below, pp. 72–74).

The west analemma consists of large, rectangular blocks that vary between 0.85 m and 1.80 m in length and 0.67 m to 0.85 m in width, smoothly finished only on the outer face. Following the rise of the ground to the west, the first course was stepped up five times, and at each step the blocks overlap except at the point of the bend (Fig. 33). The courses vary in height from 0.35 m to 0.53; eight courses are represented in all, although only the top three continued for the full length of the wall. The homogeneity of material and workmanship throughout indicates that the entire analemma was constructed at one time. No mortar or clamps were used, and the joints are tight but not regularly spaced. Deep shifting notches occur on the top of some of the blocks, though their spacing gives no clear idea of the arrangement of the next course. The rough and irregular cutting of the anathyrosis and the finishing of the surfaces are indicative of Roman workmanship, and there is little doubt that the analemma belongs to that period.

Three buttresses, bonded into the wall, were placed at intervals along the upper section (Fig. 34). They are preserved only in the first course, and from west to east they measure 0.60 m by 0.91 m, 0.60 m by 0.89 m, and 0.64 m by 0.91 m.[4]

On the east side of the cavea all but two blocks of the analemma have been removed from the foundation trench, which is preserved for a distance of 11.40 m. Stepped cuttings along the course of the footing trench show that the wall followed the rise of the ground in the same way as on the west side and that the blocks were roughly of the same size. No evidence of an upper extension of the analemma can be discerned on the clay surface of the hill that slopes gradually down to the north.

---

times (e.g., theaters at Priene, Delos, and Athens). But that Greek analemmata were replaced with new walls of only a slightly different orientation as at Isthmia is noteworthy. Other features of a Greek character will be noted in this chapter and the next, and for this reason it will often be more relevant to compare Isthmia to theaters of Greek design rather than to theaters built or remodeled on a purely Roman plan.

4. Buttresses supported the analemmata at Corinth belonging to the reconstruction of about A.D. 14 (Stillwell, *Theatre*, pp. 47–49, 135) and at Segesta (Bulle, *Untersuchungen*, pp. 110 ff., Pl. 19); they are also found at Oropos, Athens, and Morgantina on analemmata from the Greek period.

Where the outside rim of the new cavea would have fallen on the west side, a short stretch of foundation is preserved, 2.00 m long and 1.08 m wide (Fig. 34, far right foreground; Pl. II), and two blocks with traces of a second course are found on the same line farther south (Pl. I). The eastern or inside face of the blocks is finished; on the outside they project unevenly. These foundations may have been the beginning of an outside wall for the cavea, with a corridor planned around the edge just inside the wall. Inasmuch as no other remains of the wall have been found, the project appears to have been abandoned in its early stages.

The lower section of the seats was again refashioned, this time with nine rows of steplike cuttings that supplied foundations for seat blocks and a step at the bottom arranged in a continuous curve (Figs. 5, 19). The earlier seat blocks had very likely been removed when the sanctuary was first abandoned, and in their absence the clay foundations of the cavea must have been heavily eroded by the weather. Therefore, new foundations were needed for the new seats, which in turn have all disappeared with the exception of one slab found lying on end in the west parodos (see below, p. 68).

Foundations of stone had to be supplied for the last three rows of seats on the east side and for two rows on the west because the hill falls away at the sides. Of these, two blocks are in place on the west side, and one of them bears a cutting for the back edge of a seat block. The cutting for a third such block appears a little to the south.

The steplike foundations for the seats vary in width between about 0.50 m and 0.80 m, and they have an average height of 0.31 m. The seat blocks apparently were not finished to a uniform width, but when they were installed the clay was cut back to fit each block separately.[5] Where necessary, earth and poros chips were packed behind the blocks, and some of this packing is still in place, especially in the central and eastern sections.[6]

The virgin clay at the top of the seat foundations on the central axis is 2.52 m above the proskenion sill; at the east it descends to +1.50 m and on the west to +1.87 m, which reflects the natural contour of the hillside (Pl. II). The top surface of each row slopes gently downward toward the center of the row on the axis, with a total drop of about 0.06 m on the east side and 0.10 m on the west. This incline is so consistent in each row, in-

5. It is easier to cut clay than stone, and the seats in the odeum at Corinth were arranged in much the same manner. In some areas the soft hardpan was cut to fit the rear faces of the seat blocks and in others additional packing was added. See O. Broneer, *The Odeum*, Vol. 10 of *Corinth: Results of Excavations Conducted by the American School of Classical Studies at Athens* (Cambridge: Harvard University Press, 1932): 12, Pl. II.

6. Lime mortar was not used in these foundations or elsewhere in the cavea at this time. Its absence is characteristic of construction in the first Roman period as seen in the wings of the scene-building and the first northeast building (below, pp. 75, 84).

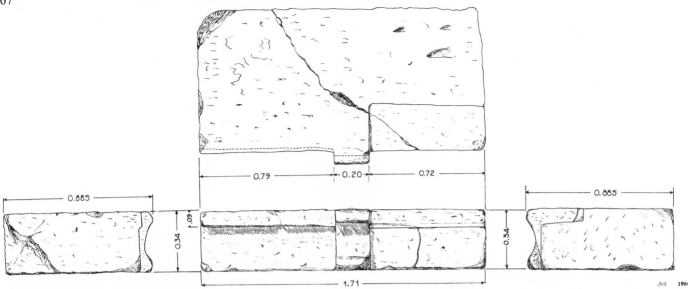

Fig. 35. Drawing of seat block from Roman cavea.

Fig. 36. Seat block from Roman cavea.

creasing slightly in the upper rows, that it appears to have been an intentional part of the design. If the slope was carried out in the stone seats, it would have helped to channel rain water to the center of the cavea for drainage through the orchestra.

The only seat block found during the excavation lay in the western end of the west parodos. It is a block of poros limestone, 1.74 m long, 0.86 m wide,[7] and 0.34 m high (Fig. 35). The seat proper, 0.79 m long, is finished with a console that separates it from a rudely cut step on the other end of the block (Fig. 36). Along the front of the seat block runs a simple taenia, 0.09 m high, a rather unusual feature for a Roman seat.[8] At the back of the seat block a band of unweathered surface, about 0.12 m wide, shows where the block was covered by the seat above (Fig. 35). The width of the entire row, including seat and footrest for the row above, would thus have been about 0.70 m.[9] The step has a shallow rise of only 0.09 m and is very roughly cut. The lower tread is also quite narrow, about 0.28 m, leaving 0.42 m for the upper tread. The first arrangement probably provided steps of the same height as the seats, but later small additional treads were cut into the lower part of at least one step. (Smaller steps for all the stairways have been indicated on the restored plan; see Pl. VIII.) Since virtually no curve is distinguishable on the front of this seat block, it must have been located at one wing of the cavea where the curve flattened out to almost nothing. Furthermore, it must have been on the west wing because the stairway would have run along the inside of the analemma.[10]

That the lowest of the foundation cuttings for the seats is considerably narrower than the others is clearly visible in spite of the many irregularities in the clay. From this it is probable that a step or footrest ran around the bottom of the cavea. At its narrowest point the foundation is about 0.40 m wide, which represents the approximate width of the step. Its forward edge would have overlapped slightly the blocks along the edge of the orchestra (see below, pp. 70f.), and at the back it would have received the front edge of the first rows of seats.

The foundation cuttings can provide no information concerning the placement of the stairways since the steps were cut into the same blocks as the seats. On the restored plan (Pl. VIII), a suitable number of stairs separating the *kerkides* have been drawn, based on the size of the cavea.

On the one remaining seat block there are no lines to mark the space allotted to each spectator, although a seat 0.79 m long would surely have

7. The clear width not including projection of the curved member is 0.82 m.

8. Dilke, *BSA* 43 (1948): 192.

9. This is the same width as that estimated for the rows of the Greek cavea. It is normal for Roman seat blocks to have no division between the seat and footrest behind.

10. The block has been set up by the excavators in the second row next to the west analemma.

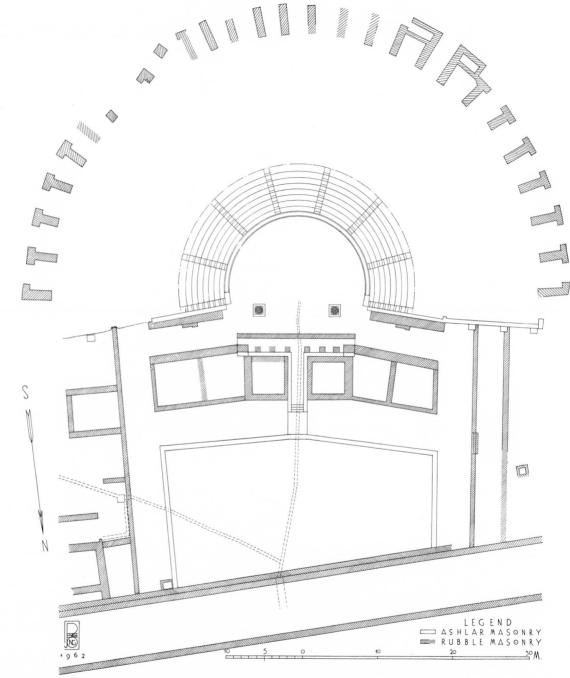

LEGEND
☐ ASHLAR MASONRY
▨ RUBBLE MASONRY

S

N

1962

0   5   0   10   20   30 M.

Pl. VIII. Second Roman period, restored.

accommodated more than one person. At Corinth a space of 0.36 m was assigned to each spectator,[11] and at Athens it was about 0.41 m;[12] at Pompeii the theatergoer had a seat 0.39 m wide; in the amphitheaters at Nîmes and Arles it was 0.40 m.[13] If a seat of about 0.39 m, which is the mean, were allotted to each spectator at Isthmia, the eight rows of permanent seats would have accommodated about 868 persons.[14] This is a small number considering the crowds that must have attended the Isthmian games, and we must suppose that temporary wooden seats were erected on the upper slope where an extension of the cavea had been projected.

The slope of the cavea was increased in the Roman remodeling, from a rise of 1:3.20 m to 1:2.72 m.[15] To steepen the unusually shallow incline of the Greek auditorium may have been one of the reasons for completely recutting the cavea, a thing that was rarely done in the remodeling of a Greek theater (see above, p. 66). An outstanding example of remodeling had been completed at Corinth a few decades earlier,[16] and it may have provided the impetus for a similar project at Isthmia.[17]

The Orchestra

When the cavea was rebuilt, the shape of the orchestra was changed from an inverted U-shape or arched-window form to one with a curve of about 214°, flattened at the ends and following the line of the seats. Its area was also enlarged, and the inner radius was extended about 1.90 m (to a total length of 8.80 m) with the removal of the paved walk and the first four rows of seats. In order to establish a new floor, the cutting and bedding for the stone border from the Greek period were filled in with poros chips and hard-packed earth; this layer of packing was uncovered all along the edge of the orchestra during excavation (Figs. 20, 21, 23). Among the very few sherds in this upper layer was a small red-glazed fragment of the first century A.D. (chap. 2, p. 36).

Around the edge of the new orchestra a shallow bedding was cut into the clay, 0.75 m to 1.10 m wide and now only 0.03 m to 0.06 m deep along

11. Stillwell, *Theatre*, pp. 31–32.

12. Dilke, *BSA* 45 (1950): 22.

13. J. Formigé, *Rémarques Diverses sur les Théâtres Romains* (Paris: C. Klincksieck, 1914), p. 8.

14. When allowance has been made for eight stairways, each 0.72 m wide, the space on the eight rows of permanent seats would have measured a total of about 338.42 m. If the Corinthian standard of 0.36 m per spectator, instead of 0.39 m, were used, another seventy-two persons could have been accommodated, bringing the total to 940 persons.

15. Likewise the cavea of the Corinthian theater was steepened, from a rise of 1:3.08 m to one of 1:2.08 m in the Roman period (Stillwell, *Theatre*, pp. 26, 46).

16. The first remodeling of the theater at Corinth occurred between the end of the Augustan period and the early years of Tiberius' principate (ibid., pp. 45–49, 135).

17. The whole sanctuary appears to have suffered a decline, if not total abandonment, while its patron city lay in ruins. Cf. Broneer, *Klio* 39 (1961): 253; *Isthmia I*, p. 101.

its inner edge. The outer edge, about 0.30 m high, bordering the first step of the cavea, is cut in notches and jogs in the same manner as the cuttings for the seat blocks, and in the rear are sections of packing still clinging to the clay. The bedding was clearly intended to receive blocks forming a stone border at the outer limit of the orchestra, with an exposed width of about 0.65 m.[18] The border began 1.40 m from the analemma at each side.

A gutter channel may have been cut into the stone border around the orchestra, although there is little evidence of any connection between the border and the central drain, which was new or completely redone at this time. With an edge of about 0.10 m on each side, the channel itself could have been only about 0.45 m wide, and with the allowance of 0.10 m for the bottom, its depth would have been 0.20 m, deepening to 0.31 m at the east end where the bedding slopes downward.[19]

According to the slope of the foundation cutting, the water would have been directed toward the east end of the channel, but the single inlet to the drain in its present condition is a small opening near the center of the orchestra, about 3 m south of the proskenion sill (Pl. I; see below, pp. 80 f.). The only clues to a link between the opening and the gutter are the fragments of terra-cotta pipe found around the inlet and the broken roof tiles that appeared in some quantity over the entire area between the drain and the east end of the gutter. A pipe protected by roof tiles may have been located here, or a channel lined with tiles.[20]

In the face of such fragmentary evidence the possibility that the theater continued without a gutter throughout Roman times cannot be discarded. In that case the series of blocks surrounding the orchestra would have formed a narrow walk for the spectators, similar to the stone border and walk of the Greek period.[21]

The orchestra floor, presumably of hard-packed earth, has perished, as it has from all other phases of the Isthmia theater. If, as seems likely, the proskenion remained in something like its original form (pp. 73–74), the orchestra floor could not have risen above the sill and would not have been

18. At its narrowest point the cutting is only 0.75 m wide, and a minimum overlap for the joint between the first step of the cavea and the blocks would have been about 0.10 m. See the late Roman gutter at Corinth that has a very irregular outer edge concealed under the first row of the cavea (Stillwell, *Theatre*, p. 44, Fig. 37).

19. Even some large theaters had gutters of relatively small dimensions. At Argos the rock-cut gutter in the orchestra is about 0.40 m wide and 0.30 m deep and served to drain water from the orchestra and the first six rows of seats; a larger gutter in the diazoma behind was provided for the rest of the huge cavea. The gutter at Megalopolis is 0.50 m by 0.30 m.

20. A gutter has been indicated on the restored plan (Pl. VIII), but remains of a pipe or connecting channel to the drain are too scattered for location on the plan.

21. A narrow paved walk is found at the edge of the orchestra in the large theater at Pompeii, probably added with the low marble steps for the proedria in the Augustan period (Bieber, *Greek and Roman Theater*, pp. 172–73, Figs. 606, 607). See also the theater at Ostia (ibid., p. 191, Fig. 648).

lower than the rebate on the front of the sill, a level of -0.04 m. At the other side the top of the gutter or paved walk, fixed by the level of the first step of the cavea at $-.07$ m or perhaps a little higher at the outer edge, reveals that the level of the orchestra was about the same over its entire surface and remained little changed from the preceding period.

Some adjustment was required for the inner or lower ends of the parodoi due to the fact that the first four rows of seats had been eliminated and the new analemmata ended about 2.50 m short of the earlier ones. Very likely to avoid recutting the floors of both the parodoi, the final two blocks of the first course of the Greek walls were left in place (blocks E and F, the latter represented now only by its bedding, and the blocks next to them). These would have acted as retainers for the slightly higher floor of the parodos. In addition, between blocks E and F and the ends of the gutter or walk, there may have been a short stretch of pavement of the same width as the gutter but as high as the inner end of the blocks, $+0.15$ m or 0.225 m above the gutter.[22]

The Skene

The old wooden scene-building must have been in an advanced state of disrepair; about two hundred years had elapsed since the sack of Mummius, during which period the whole sanctuary appears to have suffered a decline. The renovators would have had the option either of starting from the beginning and designing an entirely new scene-building or of salvaging whatever they could from the old one and incorporating it in their building (see above, p. 65). They apparently chose the latter because the stone retaining wall at the rear of the proskenion, the end walls of the proskenion, the walls of the central passage, and block A from the north wall of the west parodos bear remains of a coat of white stucco applied over a thick base of lime mortar.[23] The stucco can be assigned with certainty to this period because it continues behind the rectangular bases added to the proskenion in the next remodeling and it appears on block A, which was later removed together with the parodoi walls.

Work on the building was evidently still in progress when the stucco was applied to the rear wall of the proskenion as its lower edge is quite uneven, following the irregularities of the dirt floor before the final surface

---

22. The cutting for such a pavement is best seen on the west side (Pl. I). A similar stretch of pavement beyond the ends of the gutter is found at Delphi and Leontion.

23. New stucco was also used to refurbish the south stoa in the early Roman period at Corinth (Broneer, *The South Stoa*, pp. 100-101, 158). Many pieces of stucco were found in the proskenion, the central passage, and at the north side of the orchestra; none of them bears traces of painted decoration on its smooth creamy white surface.

was established.[24] Upon completion of the work, the final floor level was fixed at about +0.10 m inside the proskenion, with a gradual decline toward the center inasmuch as the passage floor was a little lower.

In the central passage there was little disturbance in later years. The walls were stuccoed to a level of −0.06 m, which equals the lower edge of the original finished surface of the wall. At about the same level sections of a hard-packed earthen floor with three shallow work *stroses* beneath it were found along the east side of the passage and slightly overlapping the blocks at the east side of the central drain (Fig. 12). Vase fragments of the mid-first century A.D. (described below, p. 84) were found beneath the hard floor. The sequence of construction seems to have been as follows: the first project undertaken at this time was the construction or reconstruction of the central drain, which necessitated digging up most of the passage floor and thereby breaking up the hard-packed floor surfaces from earlier periods. After the drain was finished and covered and while work on the skene (including the stuccoing) was being carried on, thin work floors were built up in the passage. When everything was completed, the final floor for the passage was smoothed out at a level of about −0.06 m, where it continued for a long time.[25] Periodic opening of the drain for cleaning and repair disrupted the floor levels over the drain itself, but along the east side the work *stroses* and final surface remained undisturbed.

At the north end of the passage it appears that the stairway from Greek times continued through the first Roman period. The hard floor and the stucco on the west wall stop where the first step would have abutted against the wall (Fig. 26). The extension of the passage and the present stair belong to the next phase of construction, as shown by the pottery of the second century A.D. found beneath it (chap. 4, pp. 132–33).

In the area of the proskenion it is not certain what provision was made for a platform or stage for the performers. It was necessary to make the platform floor high enough to allow free access to the central passage from beneath. There is also no evidence of foundations for a new stage projecting farther into the area of the orchestra. Further, the retaining walls of the old proskenion were standing. Thus we can conclude that the platform used at this time was equivalent in height and depth to the Greek pro-

24. The lower limit of the stucco at the back of the proskenion varies from +0.10 m at the west end where it is about 0.14 m above the original lower edge of the finished wall surface to −0.04 m farther east where it follows the earlier finish line. In many places the lower edge of the stucco turns up slightly so that it clearly represents the original lower edge and not a subsequent flaking off.

25. The construction floors as well as the final hard-packed floor surface overlap the blocks at the edge of the drain; the final floor is slightly higher than the lower edge of the stucco on the walls.

skenion.[26] Inasmuch as the theater seems to have been used primarily for musical and oratorical contests involving one or two performers (see p. 142), such a high, narrow stage would have been sufficient. Other details of its construction and decoration cannot be construed from the existing condition of the remains, but in essence the proskenion had been reconstructed.

The central section of the skene must have been completely rebuilt because damage to the earlier wooden building would have been irreparable. The basic dimensions, however, were fixed by the portions of its Greek predecessor that were incorporated in it, i.e., the central passage and the proskenion. The major change came with the addition of long wings on either end, the foundations of which are clearly visible.

The west wing on the outside measures between 11.28 m and 11.50 m from east to west and between 5.25 m and 6.20 m from north to south (Pl. I). The foundations for the north and west walls, 0.50 m and 0.60 m thick, respectively, are made with small stones set in earth mortar, some of which still remains in both walls. At irregular intervals in the north wall, five rectangular blocks, embedded in lime mortar, are set into the wall; in the west wall there is one such block and the beddings for two more (Fig. 37). These blocks seem to have been added to the original wall, probably to strengthen the building at the time of the second remodeling. (They will be described more fully in chap. 4, pp. 102–3.) The west wing is divided into two rooms (marked I and II on Pl. I) by a cross wall with foundations of the same kind of rubble masonry and earth mortar as used for the other walls and evidently contemporary with them. The inside dimensions of room I are at present 4.97 m to 5.39 m east to west, and 4.90 m north to south; room II is 4.60 m to 5.60 m by 5.20 m.

The south walls of the wings are missing, and it is not altogether clear what happened to the ramps from the Greek period except that their south wall along the parodos remained standing. The ramps may have continued in use during this time, in which case the front wall of the wings would have run along their north side in place of the earlier retaining walls that were removed (see Pl. IV; chap. 2, pp. 52–53). On the other hand, the ramps may have been incorporated into the wings so that the south wall of each wing was an upper extension of the wall along the parodos. The wings would then have projected to the front of the proskenion and a door at the sides would have given access to the platform. This is the arrangement

26. See the theater at Sparta, which first acquired a movable wooden skene and proskenion in the Augustan period (Bieber, *Greek and Roman Theater*, p. 122; Dinsmoor, *AAG*, p. 307). On Thasos the proskenion appears to have been rebuilt in Roman times (Salviat, *BCH* 84 [1960]: 316. The Greek proskenion continued in use in other theaters as well, as at Megalopolis, Elis, Priene (until the Antonine period), Magnesia (in the first Roman period), Epidauros, Eretria, Oropos, Oiniadai, and Piraeus.

Fig. 37. Concrete foundations for piers around the outer edge of the second Roman cavea, near the west end, looking southeast.

found in most theaters of Roman design, where projecting rooms *(para-scaenia)* were placed at the ends of the scene-building.[27] It is perhaps the most probable alternative here, in view of the fact that the foundation cuttings for the earlier walls at the north side of the ramps were filled with hard-packed clay and there are no foundations or cuttings for new walls.

The appearance of the east wing would have been essentially the same as the west wing, but even the rubble foundations here have almost completely disappeared. The bedding for the east wall is visible, and one of the rectangular blocks in the north wall, with cuttings for two more, is preserved. A large clay pit occupying the eastern side of the wing may account for the disappearance of the interior cross wall; a cross wall is restored in the plan (Pl. VIII) on analogy with the west side.

The design of the wings was influenced by several elements outside of the scene-building. The north and south walls of the west wing were laid out approximately parallel to the eastern (lower) section of the west analemma and the partition wall was placed at right angles to them. The west wall of the wing was oriented with reference to the western (upper) part of the analemma and perpendicular to it (Pl. I). In the east wing the same is true of the north and south walls; they are approximately parallel to the western (lower) section of the east analemma. In the absence of an

27. See the odeum of Herodes Atticus in Athens, the theaters at Ostia, Orange, Merida, Timgad, Sabratha, Aspendus, and others (Bieber, *Greek and Roman Theater*, pp. 190–213).

upper extension of the analemma on this side, the end wall is located roughly at right angles to the other two walls. This apparent dependence of design on the plan of the cavea would be an indication that the work on the scene-building was done after the cavea was laid out, as seems also to have been the case in Greek times.

In the northeast corner of room I, a circular depression in the clay was presumably filled in at the time that the wing was constructed. The cavity contained a small red bowl (Fig. 38), some sherds of the first century A.D., and the fragment of a type XVI lamp, which will be described below in the section on chronology (p. 85), since they were probably left there during construction.

Many palmette antefixes were found in the area of the theater, and there are a total of sixteen types represented. In all but two cases, however, only one or two representatives of each type were recovered, and therefore they must have found their way into the theater from other buildings. Of the two types that occur most frequently, one is considerably more numerous and very probably belongs to the second Roman scene-building. The eleven examples of the other type (Fig. 39) can thus be assigned to the first Roman scene-building. Two of them are complete and one also retains part of a Corinthian type cover-tile on the back (IT 705).[28]

The maximum height of the antefix is 0.216 m, the maximum width

28. Two fragments of these palmette antefixes were found at stereo level beside two foundations for piers of the later Roman cavea where they must have fallen during construction of the piers. Three fragments came from the northeast area below the second Roman level, two more were found at the east end of the east parodos also below the level of the second Roman period, and many others came to light from the fill inside the central drain.

Fig. 38. Red bowl found in depression under room I of Roman scene-building (IP 2823).

Fig. 39. Palmette antefixes belonging to the skene of the first Roman period (IT 691, 705).

Fig. 40. The marble head of an Isthmian victor found in the west parodos.

0.202 m; the clay is brick red (or light buff in some examples) of a rather coarse texture. The front surface was covered with a thick coat of white-wash or paint that is at least partially preserved on most of the fragments. The palmette is composed of nine flat leaves rounded on the ends and symmetrically arranged around a triangular heart. Spirals on each side of the heart curved outward and then down to intertwine with a bottom band. At the center of each spiral is a round eye. The design is similar to Greek models from Corinth,[29] but the coarse fabric, poor whitewash, and rough finishing of the product after it left the mold are characteristic of Roman workmanship. Nevertheless, the fact that the style of the palmette reflects Greek antecedents corresponds well with the generally Greek character of the theater in the first Roman period.

The only major sculpture that escaped the final, thoroughgoing destruction of the theater was a lovely white marble head found in a hole along the north wall of the west parodos, at the east end (Fig. 60). A youth is represented at about three-quarters life size, wearing the crown made of pine awarded to an Isthmian victor. Originally the head seems to have been part of a relief, but the background is broken off and no other fragments were brought to light. The surface and features exhibit the fine workmanship and style of the first century A.D.[30]

The Parodoi

The dimensions of the parodoi changed little from those of Greek times. With the new analemmata along the south sides, the width of the western parodos at the bend must have been about 3.75 m, narrowing to 3.40 m at orchestra level; on the east side it narrowed from 3.70 m to 3.30 m. It is evident that the present ground level in the parodoi is considerably lower than it was in antiquity because the foundation trenches for the walls along the north side have been reduced to shallow cuttings visible only at the lower ends (Fig. 18), and on the south side the first course of the west analemma above the bend now rests a little above the present floor of the parodos (Fig. 33). The incline of the floor is still steep, 0.115 m to the meter, but it must have been even more pronounced in Greek and Roman times.

Beyond the entrance to the west parodos the ground rose rather steeply, and the area seems to have been free from other buildings. On the east side of the theater the terrain is more level, and there may have been a boundary wall running north and south below the cavea (see below, p. 83).

Behind the scene-building six blocks belonging to a Doric entablature

29. See I. Hill and L. King, *Decorated Architectural Terracottas*, Vol. 4, Part I, of *Corinth: Results of Excavations Conducted by the American School of Classical Studies at Athens* (Cambridge: Harvard University Press, 1929): Pl. II.

30. See Broneer, *Hesperia* 28 (1959): 326–27, Pl. 66a; idem, *AJA* 66 (1962): 259–63, Pl. 67, Fig. 4.

were found built into the second course of the west and south walls of the court that was added to the theater in the following period. Three of the blocks were reused in their original length, and the three others were cut off at one end. All but two of them rest face down so that only the rear surfaces with traces of stucco are exposed. The three complete blocks are 2.15 m, 2.24 m, and 2.26 m long, and they are uniformly 0.67 m high and 0.45 m wide. The smaller segments measure 1.025 m, 1.28 m, and 1.35 m in length with the same height and width as the others. They are of poros limestone, finished with a toothed chisel, and exhibit rather careless workmanship. On the two blocks with faces exposed the outline of triglyphs and metopes is just barely discernible since they have been largely cut away and the surface is badly weathered. On the easternmost block of the series, located toward the west end of the south wall (Pl. I; partially visible on Figs. 41, 42), the three triglyph-metope units are from 0.74 m to 0.765 m

Fig. 41. Court and crossroad along south side, looking east from the west terrace. Pipes (6) and (5) in lower right, (7) in center.

Fig. 42. West entrance road, looking south.

long and 0.285 m high. They are surmounted by a taenia 0.08 m high and an architrave 0.30 m high. One-half of a fan-tailed clamp hole is cut deep into the top of the blocks at each end, probably for a wooden clamp, and clamp holes occur also on the other complete block.[31] Patches of stucco on the bottom reveal that the blocks did not rest on a wall, but it is not clear whether the supports at either end were columns or piers. The top surface is rough where it would have received a crowning member. On the rear face of the blocks lying face down runs a fascia along the top, 0.24 m wide.[32]

The original position of these blocks in the theater, if in fact they belonged there, remains obscure; but inasmuch as they were reused in the theater court, they probably came from some structure in or near the theater that was demolished at the time of the second Roman remodeling. Since they were freestanding and of slight proportion, they could have been part of an ornamental gateway at the entrance to the parodoi,[33] or perhaps

31. For the use of wooden clamps at Corinth in the mid-first century A.D. see the odeum where they occur in the cavea and scene-building (Broneer, *Odeum*, pp. 14, 38, Figs. 14, 22). They are also found at Isthmia in the first century A.D. arch incorporated into the Northeast Gate of the so-called Fortress of Justinian and in the heavy east-west wall belonging to an unidentified complex along the ravine north of the theater, next to the Roman fortification wall (Pl. VIII).

32. The fascia cut in the block is about 0.23 m wide, but the band marked off by a groove in the stuccoed surface is 0.24 m, another sign of careless finishing.

33. Gates are frequently found at the upper entrances of the parodoi, e.g., at Oropos, Sikyon, Leontion, Segesta (as restored by Bulle, *Untersuchungen*, Pl. 19), Epidauros, and perhaps Eretria (Fiechter, *Ant. Th.*, 8: 38, Pl. 8). They are located at the ends of the proskenion at Assos, Priene, and Delos. (Continued, p. 80.)

they belonged to some larger entrance to the theater area. The columns or piers that supported them would have been too large and too high for use in a proskenion colonnade of this period.[34]

At the upper end of the west parodos stands a circular base (originally about 1.02 m in diameter), placed against the analemma just east of the bend. It was set there some time after the analemma was constructed because the buttress has been trimmed off to make room for it. On the other hand, it antedates the later parodos wall into which it was incorporated. The base is now 0.42 m high, and its top would have been close to the original ground level. It may have supported some monument placed at the entrance to the parodos.

The Central Drain

The central drain begins in the orchestra, about 3.05 m south of the center of the proskenion sill (Pls. I, II). No inlet is preserved at a level high enough to have reached the orchestra floor, and in its present state the floor of the opening lies at −0.40 m and slopes down to the north. The first section, 1.30 m long, has an earthen floor and sides made with broken pieces of tile laid horizontally in earth and resting on a ledge of clay about 0.10 m high above the floor (Fig. 43). The top was covered with flat tiles, which were removed by the excavators in order to clear the channel. At the end of the first section the construction changes; the channel widens abruptly, and the floor drops about 0.10 m, which gives the impression that the first stretch was added to the drain at a later time.

The next part of the drain, up to the proskenion sill, is made with blocks set on edge along the sides, except in the portion immediately south of the sill and under the sill where the sides are cut in clay. Two large reused blocks (one of which is half of a threshold) served as cover slabs. The channel is 0.30–0.43 m wide and 0.21–0.26 m deep. Where the drain passes under the sill it narrows slightly and is very unevenly cut.

Under the central passage the channel is again built from reused

At Isthmia, however, the clear width of the parodos entrance would have been approximately 3.70 m on the east and 3.75 m on the west, which would have accommodated five triglyph-metope units (5 × 0.74 m = 3.70 m). The main difficulty in relating the reused blocks to parodos gates is that three long blocks are preserved whereas only two long and two short would have been needed for the parodoi, and the long blocks have clamp holes at both ends.

34. The height of the architrave and frieze is 0.67 m, to which would have been added a cornice of about 0.15 m. The width of the architrave (0.45 m) calls for a column shaft about 3.78 m high, and with the capital it would have been about 4.05 m according to the proportions of 1:7 given in Vitruvius (IV. 3. 4). The Doric columns in the Roman market gate in Athens have proportions of 1:6.45 (W. Judeich, *Topographie von Athen*, Sec. III, Part II, Vol. 2 of *Handbuch der Altertumswissenschaft*, ed. W. Otto [Munich: C. H. Beck, 1931]: 371).

material. The sides are lined with blocks set on edge, and the top is covered by slabs loosely fitted together and packed with small stones, tiles, and clay.[35] In most places the blocks lining both of the sides rest on a ledge of clay that varies in height from about 0.04 m to 0.20 m above the drain floor. The construction in general is careless, although some of the irregularities are probably the result of repairs made over a long period of time. The accumulation of silt inside the channel would have necessitated a periodic removal of the cover slabs for cleaning. A repair is seen on the west side where two of the vertical joints have been patched with lime mortar, not used elsewhere in drain construction.

The peculiar way in which the side blocks rest on a ledge of clay suggests that there may have been an earlier channel cut into the clay hardpan along the same course. The stone sides would then have been put in at the time of the Roman remodeling simply by cutting down the sides of the channel without altering the bottom. The short stretch of drain under the proskenion sill would then be a remnant of the earlier channel that was never changed, very likely due to the difficulty of working beneath the sill. Another explanation for the clay ledge at the sides relates it to the cleaning process, whereby the workman who dredged the silt lowered the bottom of the drain at the same time.

35. One slab is part of a small poros architrave; another came from a stone-cut channel (0.24 m wide) lined with Greek stucco. The sides of the channel have been hacked off, and the block seems to be too narrow to have belonged to an orchestra gutter.

Fig. 43. South end of the central drain in the orchestra, looking north.

Beyond the central passage the drain continued northward under the court, dropping even farther below the ground level. A short section of it was brought to light immediately inside the south wall of the court (Pls. I, II). The lower part of the channel walls is very much like that under the passage; the blocks rest on a ledge of clay about 0.10 m above the floor, and no mortar was used between them. Where it passed under the court wall it was 0.25 m wide and 0.30 m deep. Once inside the court, however, the sides continue upward for another 0.48 m, and they are lined with small stones set in lime mortar to which a layer of lime mortar was applied to seal the inner surface. This upper section was evidently added later, perhaps in order to bring the cover slabs closer to the surface to facilitate opening and cleaning. Similar construction utilizing small stones and lime mortar is found in other parts of the theater belonging to the second Roman remodeling.[36]

One other section of drain was explored in the center of the court where it passes over the collapsed Greek cistern. The same construction in two layers continues, although the upper extension is 0.54 m high to compensate for the increased depth of the drain. At the lower level the side blocks were placed directly on the earth that had accumulated inside the cistern before or shortly after its collapse. The silt, which accumulated in the drain during its use, continued down about 0.10 m below the bottom of the side blocks. The lack of a hard bottom to the channel in this area may have allowed a drain cleaner to dredge too deeply during one of the clearing operations.

At the north end of the court the construction is again different. The drain is lined with tall and rather thin slabs, tightly fitted, that rested on a ledge of clay about 0.40 m above the floor of the channel,[37] which was 0.70 m deep and 0.28 m wide. The slabs extended the full height of the drain without any upper extension of stones and mortar. The top was covered with large stone slabs. Near the center of the court a terra-cotta pipe emptied into the drain from above, but its connections with a water source on the surface have been lost. At the north wall of the court the drain was interrupted and the blocks lining it were rudely cut off to make way for the foundations of the court wall. At the same time a new channel was constructed to carry the water through the wall and beyond (described in chap. 4, pp. 119–20). Another drain coming in from the southeast joined the central drain just inside the court. It is made of bricks and mortar and undoubtedly belongs to the later period.

36. See the foundations for the skene (center section), the second northeast building, and the parodoi walls supporting the barrel vaults.

37. The bottom of the drain was cleared only to a hard layer of earth instead of to hardpan. The hard layer was 0.40 m below the bottom of the side slabs, and it very likely marks the bottom of the channel, at least at the time of its rebuilding. The drain from the Greek

The area beyond the east end of the scene-building and stretching northward seems not to have been occupied by permanent buildings before the first Roman period.[38] In Greek times the natural slope of the hill would have continued to the north and east, and if some temporary structures were erected there at the time of the festivals, they have left no trace. When the theater was first remodeled under the Romans, additional earth was brought in to level the whole area and the first northeast building was built at the north end.[39] Slight remains of a long north-south wall have also been found, consisting of an uneven foundation trench (about 0.55 m wide) located 3.82 m east of wall d-d (Pl. I). It begins at the north wall of the storeroom[40] and continues northward for 10.07 m where it makes a right-angle turn to the west. The trench is too narrow and irregular for a wall of any height, and the absence of a cement bedding makes it uncertain whether the wall was made of blocks or rubble masonry like the wings of the skene. At the time of the second Roman building or before, the wall was removed and the trench filled in. The wall may have originally served or been intended to serve as a boundary for the eastern side of the theater, before the more elaborate system of entrance roads and retaining walls was built.

At a distance of 3.75 m north of the northernmost limit of the boundary wall are the remains of two buildings that will be referred to simply as the first and second northeast buildings because their actual use is unknown. The two sets of foundations are made with small, irregular stones, but they are readily distinguishable since one employs earth mortar and in the other the stones are set in lime mortar. The foundations with earth mortar are earlier, as shown by the fact that in some places they are partially covered by the others; elsewhere they lie side by side (Pl. I, where the walls in which earth mortar is used are rendered in outline).[41] A coin of Nero (Fig. 44, no. 2) was found together with some early Roman sherds near the east edge of the building below the foundations, in the earth fill that was brought

1

2

Fig. 44. Two bronze coins of Nero (enlarged); no. 1 is from the orchestra, no. 2 is from the first northeast building.

period may have continued even lower, as Greek sherds were found next to the north wall of the court at a low level. Evidence for a clay channel from Greek times is clearer here.

38. The northeast area is the section east of wall d-d (Pl. I), 8 m wide and 22 m long from the edge of the cavea to the rear wall of the so-called stoa on the north. Some of the walls and buildings in the area continue to the east, but it was not feasible to pursue them farther.

39. The nozzle of a type XVI lamp was found in this fill together with some coarse pottery of the first century A.D. For the lamp see O. Broneer, *Terracotta Lamps*, Vol. 4, Part II of *Corinth: Results of Excavations Conducted by the American School of Classical Studies at Athens* (Cambridge: Harvard University Press, 1930): 56 ff.

40. The storeroom is a small, rectangular structure at the south end of the area, and it was built during the second Roman remodeling (chap. 4, pp. 000–00).

41. The earth mortar construction closely resembles that in the wings of the skene, while the foundations containing lime mortar are similar to rooms III and IV of the second Roman scene-building.

in to level the area prior to construction. They seem to be contemporary with the first northeast building.

The south wall of the building, about 1 m thick, continued eastward beyond the excavated area. Remains of the west wall are visible along the edge of wall d-d, but it was largely destroyed when d-d was built. Little has been found of the north wall; apparently it lay at the south edge of the long wall to the north. A thin north-south partition wall, slightly bowed, divided the building, and another partition wall ran westward from it, making two small rooms. The inside measurement of the two rooms is about 4.25 m by 2.55 m. The larger room toward the east was not fully cleared since it extended beyond the area available for excavation.

Insofar as the absence of lime mortar seems to be a characteristic of the first Roman period, and the foundations with earth mortar so closely resemble those of the wings added to the skene, the first northeast building very likely formed part of the first building program under the Roman administration.

Fig. 45. Fragments from two small bowls found under the hard floor in the central passage, first Roman period. No. 1 is IP 2912, no. 2 is IP 2911.

Chronology

The date of the first Roman period can be fixed by the pottery found under the hard floor of the central passage (see above, pp. 000–00) and in the depression under the floor of the west wing of the scene-building (p. 000). A coin of Nero was found at the east side of the orchestra on the packing that covered the area of the walk around the Greek orchestra. Another coin of Nero came from the earth fill under the first northeast building.

The pottery from the central passage includes fragments of two small bowls of red fabric. One (IP 2912, Fig. 45, no. 1) has a curved profile and an original diameter of about 0.10 m; the fabric is buff-red, and the outside is covered with a red glaze of the same color. It is Pergamene ware that began to be produced about A.D. 35 to 40 and continued into the time of Nero, around A.D. 65.[42] The other fragment (IP 2911, Fig. 45, no. 2) is from a slightly larger bowl with an angular profile. The fabric is very hard, reddish buff, and the slightly rough surface is covered with red paint. It appears to be imported ware, perhaps Italian, from the reign of Claudius. None of the other fragments found beneath the hard floor seems to be later than the middle years of the first century A.D.

42. John W. Hayes of the Royal Ontario Museum kindly examined all the Roman pottery from the theater, and the opinions expressed here are his unless otherwise indicated.

The circular depression under the floor of the west wing also yielded a number of sherds from the same period, including almost all of the fragments of a red bowl (IP 2823, Fig. 38), the bottom of a Pergamene vessel, and the nozzle of a type XVI lamp (IP 2710).[43] The red bowl, 0.12 m in diameter and 0.053 m high, is made of hard red clay and is covered inside and out with red glaze. The rim curves inward, and there is a low ring base. The fabric is unusual, probably imported, although the shape is a common one from the Hellenistic period.[44] A smaller but very similar bowl was found at Corinth during the early excavations of the site.[45] A mid-first-century date is probable for the bowls, rather before A.D. 50 than after.[46]

The coin of Nero found at the east side of the orchestra (Fig. 44, no. 1) is little worn. The head of Nero occupies the obverse, bare, facing left, with the inscription NERO CLAVD CAES AVG around the edge. The reverse has a pine wreath enclosing the word ISTH MIA written on two lines and the inscription COR TI CLAVDIO OPTATO II VIR around the outside. The coin was clearly struck at Corinth in the time of Nero under the duovir T. Claudius Optatus, but the date of his administration is not recorded. However, the imperial portrait closely resembles that on the *aurei* and *denarii* of the Tr[ibunicia] P[otestas] V to VIII (A.D. 58/59 to 61/62) and very likely belongs to the same period.[47] Nero is shown as a young man with a lean face and neck, which is in strong contrast to his later coin portraits with their conspicuous heaviness of face, chin, and neck and often the addition of a slight beard.[48] During his early years as emperor the coin portraits represent Nero "as a young man of about seven-

43. Broneer, *Terracotta Lamps,* pp. 56 ff., Fig. 25, No. 230. This fragment is from group 3 of type XVI.

44. See H. Thompson, "Two Centuries of Hellenistic Pottery," *Hesperia* 3 (1934): 435–37, Fig. 117, No. A20.

45. The bowl is on exhibit in the Corinth museum (CP 418); it is 0.37 m high and 0.076 m in diameter.

46. Henry S. Robinson of Case-Western Reserve University also kindly examined the bowl and concurred with Mr. Hayes about its foreign origin and first-century date.

47. This information was graciously furnished me by David MacDowall, who has recently completed a monograph on *The Aes Coinage of Nero* (forthcoming). He notes that Ti. Claudius Optatus and his colleague C. Julius Polyaenus are the second of the four colleges to strike under Nero, and the portrait on their coins is older than that on the coins of the duoviri M. Ac. Candidus and Q. Ful. Flaccus, who would have struck *aes* coinage before A.D. 62. He adds that the eastern mints clearly did strike *aes* coinage during the first ten years of Nero's reign, although it appeared at Rome only after the reforms of 64. Cf. K. Edwards, *Coins,* Vol. 6 of *Corinth: Results of Excavations Conducted by the American School of Classical Studies at Athens* (Cambridge: Harvard University Press, 1933): 7, Class XXII. The Isthmian coin corresponds to No. 62 on Plate II, although it is better preserved. The original work on Corinthian coinage of the duoviri was done by E. Fox, "The Duoviri of Corinth," *JIAN* 2 (1899): 89–116. For our type, see his p. 113, no. 57, Type XXI. See *BMC, Corinth,* nos. 565–66.

48. See E. Sydenham, *The Coinage of Nero* (London: Spink and Son, Ltd., 1920), pp. 9–13.

teen, bareheaded . . ."[49] This corresponds well to our coin representation and, although the Isthmian coin was struck in the provincial mint at Corinth and the portrait exhibits a hard, dry rendering of face and hair, as far as age and weight are concerned it can be expected to reflect the same general head type as the imperial issues.

The other bronze coin of Nero (Fig. 44, no. 2) was found in the artificial fill below the floor level of the first northeast building. It is extremely well-preserved and shows almost no signs of wear. The head of the emperor is laureate, facing left, and there is a slight beard extending over his cheek, chin, and neck. It is very carefully modeled, and the details are delicately worked. Of the title only . . . AVG GERMAN[icus] is preserved. On the reverse the emperor, togate, is standing on a *suggestum*, facing left, his right hand outstretched. On either side of the figure are the words AD LO(cutio) AV G[usti]. The inscription around the edge reads COR L RVT PISONE II VIR QVIN. The reference to the duovir L. R. Piso and the *quinquennium* make it possible to date the coin to the quinquennial year of A.D. 67/68 when Piso together with P. Memmius Cleander were duoviri at Corinth.[50] The *adlocutio* of the emperor may well have been his speech of liberation to the Greeks that he delivered at a special celebration of the Isthmian festival on 28 November, probably in A.D. 66.[51] At the

49. Ibid., p. 10. Sydenham attributes the issues of Optatus and Polyaenus to A.D. 67 on the supposition that the Isthmian wreath commemorated Nero's victories in the games. However, the imperial image portrays a much younger Nero than is shown on the Corinth type of Piso and Cleander dated to A.D. 67/68 (p. 107). It is unlikely that they belong to the same period.

50. Edwards, *Coins*, p. 7, Class XXIII. No. 64, seems to correspond except that the emperor holds a scroll in his raised right hand and Piso's colleague, Cleander, is named instead in the inscription; see Fox, *JIAN* 2 (1899): 114–15, nos. 58, 59; *BMC, Corinth*, no. 569.

51. The text of the address with the date 28 November and reference to the thirteenth year of the emperor's tribunician power is preserved in an inscription from Acraephiae in Boeotia (*IG* vii. 2713; Dittenberger, *SIG*[3], 814). Furthermore, Suetonius describes the event: Nero "decedens deinde provinciam universam libertate donavit" (*Nero*, xxiv, 2). The year cited in the inscription would be A.D. 66 according to the revised series of Nero's tribunician years, but Suetonius characterizes him as *decedens* or departing when he gave the speech, which would place it in A.D. 67. This discrepancy and the confusion attending Nero's tribunates has led to much discussion concerning the date; did he do this grand act upon his arrival in Greece to insure a satisfactorily effusive reception at the games as well as from motives of philhellenism, or did he do it just before his hurried departure, shortly after the inauguration of the canal through the isthmus, in thanks for the warm treatment he had received? Many authorities prefer the latter alternative with the date of A.D. 67, the more recent ones following M. Hammond who regards the designation of the thirteenth tribunate in the inscription as a mistake on the part of the copyist ("The Tribunician Day during the Early Empire," *Memoirs of the American Academy at Rome* 15 [1938]: 28 f.

On the other side, A. Momigliano believes the year to have been A.D. 66 on the basis of J. Vogt's discovery that Sardinia had already become a senatorial province by 1 July 67 to compensate the Senate for the loss of Achaia (A. Momigliano, "Nero," in Vol. 10 of *the Cambridge Ancient History* [12 vols.; Cambridge: The University Press, 1934]: 735–37; J. Vogt, *Die alexandrinischen Münzen* [Stuttgart: W. Kohlhammer, 1924], pp. 34–35, n. 137).

same time he very likely won the prize in the contest of singing to the harp and in that of the heralds.[52] Pseudo-Lucian also mentions that, although competitions in tragedy and comedy were not customarily part of the Isthmian program, Nero instituted a contest in tragedy in order to win the victory.[53]

Another occasion on which Nero almost certainly visited Isthmia was when he inaugurated a project to cut a channel through the isthmus. He not only began the project with a golden shovel, he blessed it by singing a hymn to Poseidon and Amphitrite and a short song to Melikertes and Leucothea.[54] With the exception of the speech of liberation that Suetonius specifically notes was *e medio stadio*, the other performances of Nero probably took place in the theater where he would have had the best acoustical and decorative surroundings for his appearance. The coins and pottery found in connection with the constructions of the first Roman period substantiate the fact that the theater underwent a thorough refurbishing about this time, and none of the material is later than his reign. The coin of 67/68 found under the first northeast building would be an indication that some construction continued also after his departure.

He is supported by M. Levi (*Nerone e i suoi tempi* [Milano: Istituto editoriale Cisalpino, 1949], pp. 210–12) and P. Meloni (*L'Amministrazione della Sardegna da Augusto all'Invasione vandalica* [Rome: L'Erma di Bretschneider, 1958], pp. 22–24). Meloni points out that despite all other considerations, the change in the administration in Sardinia, which was directly connected to the act of liberation, must be subsequent to that act. In note 41 he summarizes the relative bibliography.

From a numismatic point of view, the emperor's speech at the end of A.D. 66 would have been a suitable subject for a reverse in 67/68 as was his *adventus* that also appears on coins of Piso and Cleander. It might also be noted here that the use of two years of the Christian calendar to designate a single year in antiquity is customary when the ancient year began at a time other than 1 January. Its use by Edwards, e.g., A.D. 67/68 *Coins*, pp. 4–7, raises the question of when the official year in Corinth began, and whether it coincided with the Roman year commencing 1 January or with a Greek calendar year beginning at some other time. MacDowall also agrees that the *adlocutio augusti* very likely represents Nero's speech of liberation, which was certainly the outstanding event of his visit from a Greek viewpoint.

52. Philostratos, τὰ ἐς τὸν Τυανέα Ἀπολλώνιον, iv. 24. See Dio Cassius, lxii. 9: Suetonius, *Nero*, xxiii.

53. *Nero sive de fossione Isthmi*, 9. However, Philostratos (v. 7) mentions the institution of a new contest in tragedy only at Olympia, and makes the odd statement that the project for cutting the isthmus occurred in the sixth year of Nero's reign, A.D. 60.

54. Pseudo-Lucian, *Nero*, 3 "Προελθὼν δὲ τῆς σκηνῆς ὕμνον μὲν Ἀμφιτρίτης τε καὶ Ποσειδῶνος ᾗσε καὶ ᾆσμα οὐ μέγα Μελικέρτῃ τε καὶ Λευκοθέᾳ." The text has been recently translated as "He advanced from his tent and sang . . ." by M. Macleod in Vol. 8 of *Lucian* in the *Loeb Classical Library* (Cambridge: Harvard University Press, 1967), as it was many years ago by E. Talbot, who rendered it "Néron sortit donc de sa tente . . ." (*Oeuvres Completes de Lucien de Samosate* 2 [2 vols.; Paris: Librairie Hachette, 1903]: 517. The introduction of a tent here seems gratuitous, and a reference to the skene of the theater at the nearby Sanctuary of Poseidon would be more probable. "He came out from the skene and sang . . ."

4

The Second Roman Period

In the final reconstruction the Isthmian theater was evidently so enlarged and embellished that it attracted the eye of Pausanius, who wrote: θέας δὲ αὐτόθι ἄξια ἔστι μὲν θέατρον . . . (ii. 1. 7). Although all of the exterior finishing, sculptures, and ornaments have been stripped away and the structures reduced to their foundations, there is evidence of an extensive building program sometime after the middle of the second century A.D.

The enlargement of the cavea was again undertaken and again left unfinished. The scene-building fared better with a complete rebuilding of the central portion and reinforcement of the wings; union between cavea and skene was achieved through vaults over the parodoi. In the orchestra rose two monumental Ionic columns, adding to the decorative effect of the new skene. A large open court was laid out north of the scene-building, and entrance roads along the sides gave access from the north. Terraces on the west side and at least two new buildings on the east expanded the complex still further. Some construction, perhaps a stoa, was begun along the north of the court, but this too appears to have been abandoned short of completion. Only additional excavation can reveal the development of the land north, east, and west of the theater, which probably took place at this time.

The Cavea

The lower section of the cavea comprising the first eight rows of seats seems to have undergone no major alteration, but work was again begun on an upper extension to increase the seating capacity. Foundations for piers, probably twenty-eight in number,[1] were laid out in a semicircle at the top of the theater slope as the beginning of a series of barrel vaults to support the seats (see below, p. 90).

The majority of the foundations are well preserved, and many of them are undisturbed (Pl. I, Figs. 2, 37, 46). Most are made of hard concrete that has a high proportion of small stones, a few fragments of pottery and roof tiles, and scattered pieces of marble with lime mortar as the binding agent. The foundations are approximately 1 m wide; the sixteen T-shaped ones have a smooth top that is about 2.20 m long. On all the foundations *in situ* the surface is horizontal, and there is no indication that construction was ever carried above the existing level. Because of this and the fact that no great masses of broken concrete are lying in the vicinity of the theater, it is clear that the cavea was never completed in concrete. The absence of an upper extension of the eastern analemma and other foundations necessary to support raised seats precludes completion in any other material and indicates that the projected enlargement was never more than begun.

1. The remains of twenty-seven piers are visible. However, the space between the eighth and ninth piers from the east end is large enough for another pier at that point, which would have brought the total to twenty-eight.

Fig. 46. Rooms IV and V of Roman scene-building, looking south. Note blocks inserted in north wall of room V, in lower left corner. Foundations for cavea piers in background.

The top surfaces of the pier foundations follow the contour of the hill. At the west end the first pier lies 3.77 m above the orchestra; the center pier near the axis is at a level of +7.31 m, and the final pier at the east end drops to +3.00 m.

Upon comparison with Roman theaters where the cavea was completed, the intended function of these foundations is clear.[2] They were planned to support the rib walls that would have carried sloping barrel vaults on which the seats would have rested.[3] The projections of the T (about 0.60 m long) at the top would have supported arches separated by decorative pilasters, which explains why the two final piers have a projection only on their inner side. The arrangement of arches and piers is well illustrated by the theater at Ostia where this portion of the cavea has been reconstructed.[4] In the center section of the Isthmian cavea the foundations are not as well preserved, but the side projections making a T shape are

2. T-shaped piers are found in the odeum at Corinth (Broneer, *The Odeum*, pp. 20–21, Pl. I) and in the theaters at Ostia (Bieber, *Greek and Roman Theater*, Fig. 647) and at Minturnae (ibid., Fig. 652). In most cases T-shaped foundations supported the inner rib walls of the cavea, while the outer circumference was encircled by a vaulted corridor. At Isthmia, however, there is no evidence of projected outer corridor, perhaps because of its small size.

3. For examples of this see Bieber, ibid., pp. 184–85, 190 ff.

4. Shops were originally housed beneath the vaults of the cavea where they faced the street; see G. Calza and G. Becatti, *Ostia* (Rome: Istituto Poligrafico dello Stato, 1955), pp. 25–26, and Bieber, *Greek and Roman Theater*, Fig. 649.

obviously missing. Of the bases in place (nos. 13 through 17 from the west end), none seems to be precisely on a radius of the cavea arc, and they are turned slightly so that they lie more nearly parallel to each other. What purpose this was intended to serve is not apparent except that it would have made the spaces between the piers more regular. A series of store-rooms or shops beneath the seats may have been planned, as has been suggested for the odeum at Corinth where a similar change in orientation of the piers is evident.[5]

Where the edge of the cavea passed over the forecourt of the western chamber of the theater cave a different kind of pier was necessary (nos. 8 and 9 from the east end, Pl. I). Heavy foundations of large, reused blocks were sunk to virgin clay for a firm bedding, and they may have risen as much as 2 m to the level of the rock ledge above the cave.

At the southwest side of the cavea two rectangular concrete foundations join two sets of piers (the 7th and 8th and the 9th and 10th from the west end, Pl. I). The western foundation is 4.05 m long and 1.75 m wide on the outside with an open space in the center; the eastern one is 4.50 m by 1.75 m. The foundations were poured at the same time as the piers. They appear to have been planned to support two stairways, back to back, that would have led to a landing giving access to the upper part of the cavea. The space between piers 8 and 9 would have constituted a passage leading under the stairs into an annular corridor and thence to the *vomitoria*. A double stairway of this kind can be seen in the odeum at Corinth[6] and in the amphitheater at Pompeii where also an ancient wall painting provides an excellent view of its original state.[7] Above the theater, foundations for a gateway at the north end of the stoa along the east side of the sanctuary probably mark the beginning of a formal passage that connected the sanctuary with the theater and other buildings in that direction (Pl. IX).

From the pier foundations, then, the arrangement of the new cavea is clear, and it is equally clear that it never progressed beyond the foundations. As in Greek times, some type of wooden seating was probably provided when the size of the crowd required it.[8]

The Orchestra

The orchestra floor seems to have remained substantially unchanged. Since blocks E and F were not removed, no lowering of the floor is likely, and it could not have risen substantially without affecting the gutter.

5. Broneer, *The Odeum*, p. 21, Pl. I.

6. See ibid., p. 32, and n. 1. This type of stair occurred also in the theater at Nicopolis (A. Neppi Modona, *Gli Edifici teatrali greci e romani* [Florence: Leo Olschki, 1961], p. 153).

7. Bieber, *Greek and Roman Theater*, p. 179, Fig. 624.

8. The use of wood in provincial theaters was not uncommon, especially in Belgium, western Germany, and the southwest of England (ibid., p. 202).

An addition to the orchestra consisted of two large bases located 2 m south of the proskenion sill, about 8 m apart and equally distant from the central axis (Pl. I, Figs. 1, 18). The eastern base is composed of two rectangular poros blocks of approximately equal size with an overall measurement of about 1.95 m (north and south) by 1.87 m. The northern edge of the easternmost block has been roughly hacked off in the course of an unsuccessful attempt to pry the blocks out of the ground. The sides are rather evenly finished, but they were not meant to be seen above ground, and the top is at a level of −0.025 m, which would have been about even with the orchestra floor. A crudely scratched setting line was made for the joint of the two blocks in the second course (now missing), which were laid at right angles to the first course. At 0.19 m from the west edge of the base a line of stucco marks the western extent of the second course or plinth, and its eastern limit is indicated by a strip of weathered surface that extended 0.16 m beyond it. Two pry holes, one on the east and one on the west, were

Pl. IX. Ancient Isthmia.

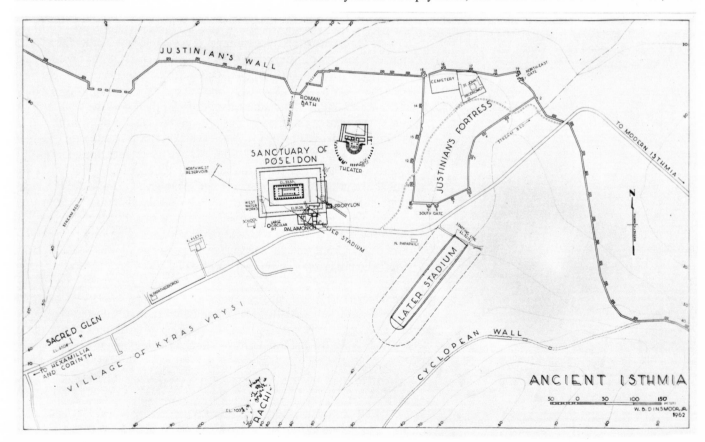

used for the second course. As closely as may be determined, the width (east-west) of the actual plinth would have been about 1.52 m, and it was probably square (Pl. I).

The western base is composed of three blocks with a total north-south dimension of about 1.91 m and 1.83 m east-west. The easternmost of the blocks was found tilted up on one side after an abortive attempt to remove it; deep grooves from the crowbars are visible in the soft stone (Fig. 18).[9] The blocks were finished like those of the eastern base, and the joint between them, exposed by the tilted block, has a well-cut anathyrosis. Here, too, there is a setting line on top for the blocks of the second course plinth, and evidence of weathering at the sides indicates that the plinth would have been about 1.55 m by 1.50 m.

When the disturbed block on the west side was raised and restored to its original position, its bedding of small stones set in lime mortar could be plainly seen and some lime mortar was evident around the edges of the blocks. As it has been noted above (chap. 3, p. 66, n. 6), the use of lime mortar appears to be limited to constructions of the second Roman period. Because of this and the more elaborate plan of the later theater, we conclude that the bases and the monuments they supported were probably installed at that time. At the corners of each base, holes about 0.23 m in diameter and 0.60 m deep were cut into the clay. Where the clay turns to sand on the west side, the sides of the holes were reinforced with tiles and stones. In all probability these holes were cut to receive scaffolding used to erect the monumental columns that stood on the bases.

Around the edges of both bases above and below ground level were a number of pieces from fillets belonging to columns of the Ionic order. The quantity and concentration around the bases leaves little doubt that columns originally stood on the bases and the fillets were either broken or cut off at the time the columns were removed. The drums of these columns, whose presence in the theater was first suspected because of the fillet fragments, were recognized in 1967 among the blocks fallen from the east wall of the so-called Fortress of Justinian, south of the northeast gate (Pl. IX, Figs. 47, 48).[10] With eleven drums were two Ionic capitals and half of an Ionic base, all of similar proportions and clearly belonging to a pair of identical columns. A twelfth drum came to light the following year. It was built into the west wall of the fortress at the place where the wall abuts the

9. The block was moved back to its original position by the excavators.

10. The drums and capitals were drawn, measured, and inventoried under the direction of Paul Clement, co-director of the Isthmia excavations in the spring of 1967. I am much indebted to Mr. Clement for permission to include this material with the study of the theater and for his great help in supplying the dimensions listed in note 13, the photographs and the drawings of the restored column (Figs. 50, 51, Pl. X), base, and capital (Pl. XI). See P. Clement, "Isthmia," Ἀρχαιολογικὸν Δελτίον 23 (1968): 140, plan 2.

Fig. 47. Ionic column drums fallen from the so-called Fortress of Justinian outside the northeast gate, looking north. One capital (IA 2011) lies at right.

Fig. 48. Close-up of Ionic column drums, IA 2003 in foreground.

south face of Tower 15 (Pl. IX) that also belongs to the trans-Isthmian wall (Fig. 49). The close resemblance both in workmanship, material, and dimensions between the fillets found in the orchestra and those on the drums securely connects the broken fillets and the columns.[11]

The columns are made from the same soft poros limestone found in the theater buildings and elsewhere at Isthmia. They were smoothly finished both with a toothed and a flat-bladed chisel, and the marks of both are readily identifiable where the surface is in good condition.[12] On most of the end surfaces where they are intact one or more lines are scored, crossing in the center at the point of a small indentation, probably made to hold the point of a compass. On one drum, IA 2003, a correction is evident. On another drum, IA 2030, there is a patch of rough, unfluted surface at one end that bears traces of a fine-textured stucco. The patch (0.25 m to 0.28 m high), covering almost one-third of the circumference (nine flutes), appears to have had a stuccoed surface, the only place where stucco was surely used on the columns. It may have been left originally for a dedicatory plaque, or a dedication may have been painted on the stuccoed surface. Its height would have been about 3.33 m above the orchestra floor, as IA 2030 is restored as the third drum in the eastern column.

The twenty-four flutes were separated by fillets between 0.017 m and 0.028 m wide; the flutes range in depth from 0.042 m to 0.058 m, and the width between the fillets varies from 0.072 m to 0.105 m, even on a single drum (IA 2003, Fig. 48). There is considerable variation in detail on all the drums and the capitals, and the workmanship is not exceptionally fine. On most drums only a few, if any, flutes are well enough preserved for complete measurements. In many places, the fillets appear to have been chiseled rather than broken off and mortar clings to the cut surfaces, showing that this was done before the drums were built into the fortress wall, probably to make it easier to fit them with other blocks (e.g. IA 2001).

The drums correspond well in terms of their upper and lower diameters. With the exception of two drums that have not yet been discovered, the twelve remaining can be restored as shown on Plate X, assembled by Mr. Paul Clement.[13] The one extant base (IA 2000, Fig. 50) has been

11. An attempt was made to discover a join between the fragments found in the orchestra and the drums, but the damaged surfaces of the latter and the difficulty of moving them to check all the flutes made it very difficult. It was noted, however, that the way in which the breaks were made on the drums corresponds to the broken edges of the fillets, and the similarity between them in texture of stone and finishing is so close that the fillets almost certainly came from these columns.

12. Where the surface was exposed to the elements, the soft stone is badly pitted and worn, and on a number of drums few or no flutes at all are preserved. This, together with their great size and weight, made measuring difficult.

13. Beginning with the first (lowest) drum in the western column, the drums have been restored in the following sequence (Pl. X) (note continues, p. 96):

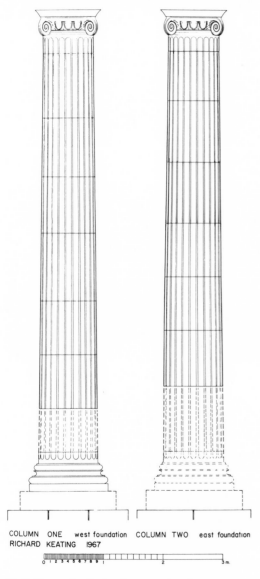

COLUMN ONE   west foundation   COLUMN TWO   east foundation
RICHARD KEATING 1967

0 1 2 3 4 5 6 7 8 9 1   2   3 m.

Pl. X. Decorative Ionic columns, restored.

Fig. 49. Ionic column drum built into the west wall of the so-called Fortress of Justinian.

A—missing; restored lower diameter 0.905 m, restored upper diameter 0.885 m, restored height 0.702 m.

IA 2005—lower diameter 0.881 m, upper diameter 0.876 m, height 0.872.

IA 2032—lower diameter 0.875 m, upper diameter 0.873 m, height 0.882.

IA 2025—lower diameter 0.864 m, upper diameter 0.856 m, height 1.085 m.

IA 2001—lower diameter 0.856 m, upper diameter 0.831 m, height 0.914 m.

IA 2007—lower diameter 0.831 m, upper diameter 0.821 m, height 0.956 m.

IA 2020—lower diameter 0.801 m, upper diameter 0.775 m, height 1.049 m.

The eastern column:

C—missing; restored lower diameter 0.910 m, restored upper diameter 0.887 m, restored height 1.120 m.

IA 2024—lower diameter 0.887 m, restored upper diameter 0.859 m, height 0.905 m.

IA 2030—lower diameter 0.854 m, upper diameter 0.830 m, height 0.872 m.

IA 2031—lower diameter 0.828 m, upper diameter 0.821 m, height 0.8666 m.

IA 68–3—diameter of one end 0.815 m, probably the lower; upper diameter, impossible to measure; height 0.905 m.

IA 2006—lower diameter 0.807 m, upper diameter 0.792 m, height 0.998 m.

IA 2003—lower diameter 0.778 m, upper diameter 0.751 m, height 0.813 m.

For IA 68–3 see P. Clement, Ἀρχαιολογικὸν Δελτίον 24 (1969): 118, Pl. 99a–b.

assigned to the western column. Its upper diameter is restored to 0.910 m and the lower to 1.324 m, which would fit well on the plinth of about 1.55 m by 1.50 m, calculated on the basis of the foundation in the orchestra. The base is of the Attic type with two torus moldings 0.087 m and 0.106 m high, above and below the scotia, respectively; the scotia is 0.072 m high. The bottom of the column ending in a narrow fillet is carved in one piece with the base. The style of the moldings follows that set in fifth-century Athens on the Erechtheion, where the top fillet of the scotia projects beyond the face of the upper torus. This, rather than the Roman variation where the fillet does not project so far, is commonly found on buildings in Greece during the empire, and a number of examples occur in Corinth. Perhaps the closest parallel to our base in profile and size belongs to Temple E at Corinth, which shows Greek influence also in its peripteral design.[14]

Both of the capitals have come to light, but in order to square the blocks for use in the wall the volutes were removed and most of the moldings. Fortunately, one complete volute and a fragment of another were found nearby, and a restored drawing of the capitals could be made (Pls. X, XI, Fig. 51). The volutes were carved on four sides with three eggs and four

14. L. Meritt, "The Geographical Distribution of Greek and Roman Ionic Bases," *Hesperia* 38 (1969): 190, 195, n. 33; Plate 50 b.

Fig. 50. Base of Ionic column (IA 2000).

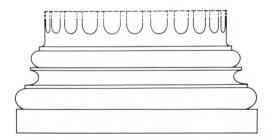

Pl. XI. Capital of Ionic column, restored.

Fig. 51. Capital of Ionic column, IA 2011.

darts on the echinus between them. A spray of four acanthus leaves extends from the spiral of the volute, reaching to the outer edges of the eggs. The capital is separated from the shaft by a torus molding 0.047 m high bordered by two narrow fillets. The abacus, about 0.113 m high, is concave in section. In the top of both capitals a Lewis hole (on IA 2011, 0.17 by 0.07 by 0.23 m deep; on IA 2010, 0.142 by 0.06 by 0.277 m deep) is the only feature. There is no sign of marks or cuttings that could have been made by a statue or its base. The surfaces are considerably weathered; the two lines on IA 2010 crossing in the center are probably guides for the cutting of the capital, as on the drums. The entire column as restored, including the base and capital, would have been 7.806 m tall, and the ratio of lower diameter to the height would have been 1:8.58.

The use of single Ionic columns as votive monuments goes back at least to the sixth century B.C. when several were dedicated at Delphi and Delos as well as at other sanctuaries. The most famous of them is that of the Naxians at Delphi that carried the statue of a sphinx. The practice continued sporadically: a pair of tall Ionic columns supported statues of Ptolemy II (ruled 283/82 to 246 B.C.) and Arsinoë in front of the Echo Colonnade at Olympia; a commemorative shaft marks the end of the Via Traiana at Brindisium; and the custom found its most monumental expression in the great columns of Trajan, Antoninus Pius (now lost except for the base), and Marcus Aurelius at Rome. Above the Theater of Dionysos at Athens two Corinthian columns of perhaps the second or third century A.D. served as choregic monuments and supported tripods.

The two columns in the orchestra were very probably intended to support statues, perhaps representing the emperor paired with a member of his family, a wealthy benefactor, or possibly Dionysos or Poseidon. And yet there is no evidence on the tops of the capitals that they ever carried such a statue, which may be one more unfinished element in the theater.

It is unusual to find such monuments in a theater orchestra, Greek or Roman, because they would have impeded the view of the scene-building and any activity in the orchestra. Smaller statue bases from the Roman period have been found at the edges of the orchestra at Priene and Delos; at Epidauros they were placed directly in front of the proskenion and in the paraskenia.[15] The fact that the large columns at Isthmia had such a prominent place in the orchestra is a further indication that use of the theater was devoted primarily to oratorical and musical contests involving one or two participants who would have appeared on the proskenion rather than in the orchestra. The columns would have provided an ornamental frame for the performer, thereby adding to the decorative effect of the new scene-building.

15. A. von Gerkan and W. Müller-Wiener, *Theater von Epidauros*, p. 81.

The Scene-Building

Among the most conspicuous remains in the theater as it stands today is the scene-building of this period. Its heavy foundations, marked III and IV on Plate I, are plainly visible on top of the clay bank where they obliterated all traces of earlier structures (Figs. 1, 2, 46). Inasmuch as only the foundations of the building are preserved and no architectural elements from the superstructure have been identified (except the antefixes from the roof), no attempt at reconstructing the façade would be useful. As far as can be ascertained, the ground plan remained very close to that of its predecessors.

The first floor of the scene-building, as in earlier periods of the theater, stood on top of the clay bank above the orchestra. In the center section the rubble masonry of the foundations is made with fist-sized stones and some fragments of pottery bound together with generous amounts of lime mortar, very much like the cavea piers and the second northeast building.[16] They are quite different from the light rubble foundations for the wings, which are made with earth mortar. Although at the present level of the remains two separate rectangular foundations are evident (III and IV, called rooms for the sake of convenience) separated by the central passage, originally the flooring would have covered the foundations and the passage and inside the building there could have been a large room 12.20 m long by 4.00 m wide (interior measurement).[17]

The rectangular foundations are approximately square. On the inside, III is 4.30 m long and 4.00 deep, and IV is 3.85 m long. The south wall of IV has completely disappeared along with its foundation trench, but the broken end of the west wall indicates that it was comparable to the south wall of III. The foundations for the west wall of III and for the east wall of IV are about 1.00 m thick, while the other foundations average about 0.74 m in thickness.[18] The concrete was poured in layers into the founda-

16. It is difficult and often misleading to assign the same names to provincial Roman masonry as those that are given to buildings in Italy on the basis of detailed descriptions and fine distinctions. It will suffice to say that the rubble masonry in the theater resembles that found at Isthmia in the Palaimonion and stoas in the sanctuary of Poseidon, and at Corinth, particularly in the monuments on the west end of the agora, e.g., the foundations of the Temple of Tyche, The Pantheon, and the Babbius monument; see R. Scranton, *Monuments in the Lower Agora and North of the Archaic Temple*, Vol. 1, Pt. III, of *Corinth: Results of the Excavations Conducted by the American School of Classical Studies at Athens* (Princeton: The American School of Classical Studies at Athens, 1951), Pls. 2, 6 (1), 8 (2), 9 (1). Noteworthy in this consideration is the discussion by J. Ward-Perkins about Roman masonry and a comparison of concrete found around Rome with that in the eastern provinces and Greece (*The Great Palace of the Byzantine Emperors*, ed. D. Talbot Rice [Edinburgh: The University Press, 1958], pp. 77 ff).

17. No central north-south wall would have partitioned this room because of the center door opening onto the stage; see Plate IV. The area is too small for three rooms.

18. In Lugli's description of *opus caementicum* in Italy he notes that the walls were made

tion trenches, so completely filling them that there was no room for additional earth or ceramic material. There are no signs on the face of the foundations that wooden forms were used to hold the concrete while it dried, and too little remains above ground to ascertain the method or material used for the upper parts.[19]

Foundation III is located over the old stream bed that had silted up long before the first theater was built (see pp. 1 ff.). For that reason these foundations were laid deeper than the others, reaching approximately 1.10 m below the present level of the scarp at the west side so that the north and west walls would rest on clay. The south and east walls are bedded for the most part on the red earth filling the foundation trench behind the ashlar retaining wall from the Greek period and behind the west wall of the central passage (Figs. 1, 24). It is evident that the retaining wall and walls of the central passage were still standing at this time and that the concrete foundations were poured directly behind them. Impressions in the concrete made by blocks of the passage wall are clearly visible.

The foundations of room IV rest on the bank where the clay is sufficiently hard to render deep foundations unnecessary. The concrete is sunk less than 0.50 m below the surface, which may be the reason for the disappearance of the south wall and its bedding when the ashlar wall in front of it was removed.[20]

From the absence of any sign of facing on the surface of the cement, it is clear that the present remains originally lay below the ground level at that time. Also, no opening for a doorway is evident in the west wall of room III or in the east wall of IV where doors would have been necessary for access to the wings. Evidently the doors and the first floor must have been at a higher level, above the present foundations that rise to + 2.00 m at their highest point.

The east and west wings (rooms I, II, and V) appear to have undergone some alteration. Earlier (chap. 3, pp. 74–75) it was suggested that the south wall of each wing was originally an upward extension of the wall along the north side of the parodos left from the second Greek period. If that were the case, the removal of the parodoi walls (see below, p. 110)

of considerable thickness, often thicker than was necessary for support, as seems to have been the case here (G. Lugli, *La Tecnia edilizia romana* 1 [2 vols.; Rome: Giovanni Bardi, 1957]: 387, §II).

19. Concrete walls were made by constructing an open framework that helped to hold the cement while drying, or a solid form into which the cement was poured; marks of the boards are often visible; see Broneer, *The Odeum*, pp. 17–19, 31, Figs. 11–13, 21; Scranton, *Lower Agora*, pp. 17–18, regarding the Babbius monument; and Lugli, *Tecnica edilizia* 1: 385 ff., Fig. 86. Lugli points out that where the ground was firm (as the clay hardpan at Isthmia), it was preferable to lay the cement directly in the footing trench without wooden forms.

20. The retaining wall now in place was constructed by the excavators to prevent erosion of the scarp.

would have necessitated the replacement of the front (south) walls of the wings. The new retaining walls for the parodoi, which were about 0.87 m thick on the east side (wall b-b, Pl. I) and 1.10 m on the west (wall a-a), would have been heavy enough to support both the vaults over the parodoi and the south walls of the wings. In the absence of any other remains of these south walls,[21] it must be assumed that they were rebuilt as part of the parodoi and rested on the same foundation as the north walls of the parodoi.[22]

In the north wall of the west wing five rectangular poros blocks were bedded in lime mortar and set into the wall (Fig. 52, Pl. I; see above, p. 74). On the outside (north) they are even with the face of the wall, but on the inside they project slightly into the hardpan, which is higher inside the building. A similar block remains in the west wall and the beddings for three more are visible, more closely spaced than in the north wall. From the fact that the blocks are set in lime mortar and that no block is found at the corner of the wing where it would be expected if the walls and blocks were contemporary, it is likely that the blocks were set into the wall when

21. The foundation trenches located along the south edge of the clay bank were described above in chap. 2, p. 52. Inasmuch as the walls related to these trenches were removed in the first century A.D., they cannot be identified with the south walls of the wings that were rebuilt a century later.

22. In purely Roman theaters the wings were often joined to one side of the parodoi vaults, as at Orange, Merida, Timgad, Sabratha, and the Odeum of Herodes Atticus (Bieber, *Greek and Roman Theater*, Figs. 675, 676, 680, 685, 694, 712).

Fig. 52. West wings of Roman scene-building with blocks inserted in the north wall (foreground), looking southeast.

it was standing and that they represent the first course of piers that were added to reinforce the light rubble walls.[23]

In the north wall of the east wing the westernmost block *in situ* (Pl. I, Fig. 46) probably belonged to a similar reinforcing member, and the lime mortar beddings for two more with remains of rubble masonry between them are preserved along the line of the wall.

The irregular spacing of the piers in the north walls on both wings may give a clue to the location of the doorways. In room I there is a space of 2.18 m between the first two piers, and after three others placed more closely together there is another gap of 2.35 m in room II. Both of the larger spacings are approximately in the center of the wall where doors would be expected. In room V not enough is preserved to give the location of all the piers. The blocks to the east of the westernmost pier may have supported a threshold.

At orchestra level the ashlar walls along the front of the clay scarp and lining the passage continued to be used as retaining walls. The passage, however, was now covered by a concrete vault, the remains of which were found inside the passage at the time of excavation. Inasmuch as no voussoir blocks or bricks appeared in the debris, the vault must have been made entirely of concrete, and many bits of the smooth white stucco that covered the inside were brought to light. No painted decoration is evident.

A new stairway was built at the north end of the central passage, outside the scene-building, and for this purpose the passage walls were extended northward for 1.20 m. The extension was made with the same ashlar type of construction as the passage walls, but the blocks were set in lime mortar. On the west side two courses are preserved and mortar on the top of the second reveals that there was at least one more course that would have brought the wall to the level of the east-west road about +1.19 m (see below, p. 122). The horizontal coursing does not correspond to that of the passage (Fig. 26), nor is the first course laid as deep. On the east side where the blocks have been removed the foundation trench is quite distinct. It was here that numerous pieces of a large amphora were found embedded in the foundation of the stair (Fig. 53). The vase, which may be dated in the second half of the second century A.D. (see below, p. 132), can have found its way there only during construction of the stair and so gives an approximate *terminus post quem* for the operation.

A large block from the first step of the stair (0.78 by 0.59 by 0.25 m high) is in place on the west side, 0.63 m north of the skene (Fig. 25). On its east end a hollow worn in the soft stone bears witness to a long period of use. A block from the second step (0.28 m high) marks the width of the tread as 0.35 m. The third and fourth steps, now missing, were supported on a

23. This may be an indication of earthquake damage at an earlier time.

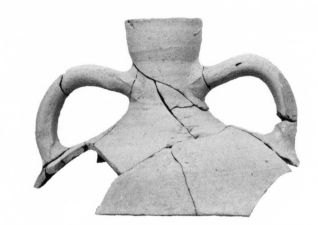

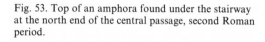

Fig. 53. Top of an amphora found under the stairway at the north end of the central passage, second Roman period.

cement foundation that retains the impression of the third step (about 0.23 m high); the fourth would have rested on top. With a height of about 0.25 m for the final step, the stairway would have ended at a level of + 1.12 m, approximately even with the side walls and the road. The side walls were continued northward to the court with cement foundations of the same thickness, apparently to support some entrance, of which nothing else remains. The short segment of the court wall that runs at right angles to the passage is a further indication of an architectural feature at this point (see below, p. 116).

At the front of the scene-building there must have been some type of proskenion or raised platform for the performers. It is quite clear, however, that there was never the kind of large, deep stage that was customary in theaters of Roman design.[24] In remodeling a Greek theater the usual procedure to achieve the required depth for such a stage was to move the front of the proskenion into the orchestra, as at Athens, Argos, Corinth, Thera, Segesta, Syracuse, Akrai, Miletus, Magnesia on the Meander, Ephesus, and Tralles. The other alternative was to place the front of the stage on the line of the proskenion and to push back the front wall of the scene-building (the *scaenae frons*), as at Priene, Sikyon, and possibly Oropos.[25] In the Isthmian theater no remains of a new wall for the stage

24. Vitruvius, v. 6. 2; see Dinsmoor, *AAG*, pp. 309–10, and Bieber, *Greek and Roman Theater*, pp. 186–89.

25. Dinsmoor (*AAG*, p. 308) includes Oropos in this category, presumably identifying wall M (see Fiechter, *Ant. Th.* 1: Pl. I) as the new front wall of the skene. Fiechter is more vague, merely labeling it as Roman (ibid., p. 23), although the only evidence is its rougher construction. P. Arnott suggests that it represents the rear wall of the first Greek scene-building because in the use of rough breccia stone it resembles the foundations of the theater of Dionysos in Athens, which are assigned to the late fifth century B.C. (*Greek Scenic Conventions in the Fifth Century B.C.* [Oxford: Clarendon Press, 1962], pp. 12–13).

front have been found in the orchestra where the ornamental columns stood instead. Nor was the front of the skene moved farther back. Thus, a deep stage was apparently never constructed, and the theater continued to have a high, narrow proskenion.[26]

At irregular intervals the proskenion sill is marked with many grooves, cuttings, and deep shifting notches that bear no relation to the earlier piers (Fig. 24), and near the east end a patch of mortar still clings to the surface. These features should very probably be attributed to a wall composed of rectangular blocks set in mortar, using the sill as a foundation. Some of the cuttings for the blocks and the weathering along the edge reveal that its outside face was set back 0.07 m from the front of the sill. The numerous pieces of undecorated white stucco found in the area would have come from the outside face of the wall. Thus, the Greek arrangement of colonnade and *pinakes* was replaced by a solid wall, but the over-all proportions of the proskenion remained approximately the same. Its depth would have been about 2.75 m[27] and its height must have continued at about 2.70 m in order to clear the top of the central passage vault.[28] It is unusual that such a high, shallow platform was built at this time, although it has earlier precedents in the Greek theaters at Segesta and Tyndaris where the proskenion façade was a solid wall with engaged pilasters or half-columns.[29] The theaters at Priene and Elis would have presented a similar appearance after the openings between the proskenion supports were walled up early in the Roman period.[30] A related form can be found in the so-called Hellenistic compromise theaters where a deep Roman stage was built with

26. This is not without parallel in other Greek theaters during the Roman period, as noted above in connection with the preceding period (chap. 3, pp. 73–74, n. 26). The difference here is that the front of the proskenion was evidently completely rebuilt, using only the original sill as a foundation.

27. The south foundation of room III may be assumed to have belonged to the front wall of the scene-building inasmuch as the ashlar retaining wall probably did not continue above the clay bank at this time.

28. A height of over 2 m is further confirmed by the fact that the proskenion floor would have agreed with the floor level of the scene-building that was above the top of foundations as they now stand, + 2.00 m. On a narrow stage such as this there would have been little room for stairways leading down to the podium from an elevated skene, as are suggested for the Roman period at Corinth (Stillwell, *Theatre*, Pl. VIIa).

29. For Segesta see Bulle's extensive study of the building, which he dates about 250 B.C. (*Untersuchungen*, pp. 110 ff., 130–31, Pls. 19, 23, 25). A. von Gerkan argues that no Hellenistic proskenion existed at Segesta (or in any Greek theater in Magnia Graecia) and the Roman stage was the first such structure ("Zu den Theatern von Segesta und Tyndaris," *Festschrift Andreas Rumpf* [Krefeld: Scherpe, 1952], pp. 82–88). For Tyndaris also see Bulle, *Untersuchungen*, pp. 131 ff. Pl. 37. Miss Bieber places both Segesta and Tyndaris around 100 B.C. and calls them "transitional" (*Greek and Roman Theater*, p. 170). Dinsmoor says "late Hellenistic" for the date (*AAG*, p. 307).

30. See A. von Gerkan, *Theater von Priene*, pp. 83–85, and Walter, *JOAI* 18 (1915): 72–74, Fig. 26.

the height of a Hellenistic proskenion.[31] At Isthmia the apparent emphasis on musical and oratorical contests would have made a large stage or elaborate apparatus unnecessary.

The end walls of the proskenion would have been dismantled down to the first course at the same time as the north walls of the parodoi were removed. Of the first course of the end walls that remained, the north half was covered by the new walls of the parodoi and the surface of the south half was cut down and shows signs of considerable wear (blocks C and D, Pls. V and VI, Fig. 11). Both ends of the proskenion were evidently left open at this point to give access to the area underneath. In order to make a level threshold for the entrance, a wedge-shaped filler was inserted on the top of block D (Pl. VI), and one seems to have been intended for C, although the cutting was not completed and packed earth may have been used instead (see chap. 2, p. 46, and n. 29 for a full description).

At the back of the proskenion on the west side are three limestone blocks spaced about 1.15 m apart and measuring 0.74 m by 0.73 m, 0.80 m by 0.73 m, and 0.80 m by 0.70 m from east to west (Pl. I). The center block, of gray stone, exhibits the characteristic rope grooves found on the blocks of the archaic temple to Poseidon;[32] the easternmost one also came from the archaic temple. The blocks rest on an uneven bedding of lime mortar and broken pieces of tile and earth so that their top surfaces are not of equal height. The stucco applied to the retaining wall during the first Roman remodeling continues behind them without interruption, which indicates that they postdate the stucco. The same series in all probability existed on the east side, but the blocks have been removed and the ground disturbed. In view of their insubstantial bedding, they cannot have supported anything very heavy, but they could have held posts to support the floor of the proskenion[33] or could represent the first course of piers that would have upheld engaged columns or statues decorating the front of

31. Dinsmoor describes and classifies these theaters: they include remodeled Greek theaters, as at Oropos, Sikyon, Priene, Miletus, Magnesia on the Meander, Ephesos, and Babylon; and the new theaters at Termessos and Sagallassus (*AAG*, pp. 308–9). They date from the first and second centuries A.D. For the latter see also D. de Bernardi, *Teatri classici in Asia Minore: 2 Città di Pisidia, Licia e Caria, Studi di Architettura Antica* (Rome: L'Erma di Bretschneider, 1969), pp. 21 ff., 54 ff., Pls. I, III, V, VIII.

32. See Broneer, *Hesperia* 28 (1959): 300; idem, Χαριστήριον 3: 64; idem, *Isthmia I: Temple of Poseidon* (Princeton: American School of Classical Studies at Athens, 1971), pp. 12–13. Mr. Broneer pointed out to me that the principal depository of building material from the archaic temple to Poseidon was the gully north of the temenos where trenches were dug for a stoa in the reign of Marcus Aurelius (see *Hesperia* 27 [1958]: 8–9, 23). At that time the blocks from the archaic temple were probably once again brought to light and made available for re-use in the theater. This also lends further support to the dating for the second Roman period (pp. 131 ff.).

33. See Segesta where Bulle conjectures that similar bases held supports for the stage or columns on the front of the skene (*Untersuchungen*, p. 122, Pls. 19, 28b).

the scene-building. If the columns or statues did exist, they would have required support from below.[34]

In the northeast and northwest corners of the proskenion were two larger bases, 1.02 m by 1.00 m and 1.02 m by 1.07 m, respectively (Pl. I). Only the mortar bedding remains on the east, but the western one is intact, incorporating two of the corner blocks (A and B) from the north wall of the west parodos and the west end wall of the proskenion (see chap. 2, p. 47, Fig. 27). Perhaps some larger form of decoration at the corners of the building called for heavier foundations. Although there was apparently no proper *scaenae frons* with deeply receding niches and columns, the front of the scene-building was very likely enhanced with some form of three-dimensional ornamentation.

Only a mere shadow of such decoration can be seen in the few fragments of marble sculpture that escaped the lime kilns. In front of the scene-building and in the orchestra the following pieces were recovered: the front of a lower, female leg with drapery attached (IS 385); more folds of drapery, similar to but not joining the first (IS 386); the calf of a leg, nude (IS 381); another piece of drapery (IS 396); a small hand (IS 401); and what seems to be a piece from a wing (IS 400). All of the fragments are small, and the human members are just under life size. They will be illustrated and described more fully in the final publication of the sculpture from Isthmia.

In summary, the scene-building at this time was 37.50 m long and 5.60 m wide, including the wings. It was very likely divided into one large center room (over foundations III and IV),[35] two rooms in the west wing, and one or two rooms in the east (Pl. VIII). A high shallow platform (about 2.70 m high by 2.75 m deep) ran across the front at orchestra level with a solid front wall facing the audience. Above the platform the wall of the scene-building was very likely decorated with some kind of sculptural ornament and perhaps columns, almost all of which has disappeared.

In the excavation of debris in the orchestra and skene so many fragments of one type of terra-cotta palmette antefix were found that it is reasonable to suppose they belonged to the roof of the scene-building during the final period of the theater. Among the twenty-one pieces that were inventoried and eighteen that were not, two variations of the same basic design are distinguishable. In one the leaves of the palmette are straight (Fig. 54), in

34. At Thasos, eight large rectangular piers were placed along the front wall of the scene-building in Roman times (C. Picard, "Fouilles de Thasos, 1914 et 1920," *BCH* 45 [1921]: 109–10). A plan appears in G. Daux and A. Laumonier, "Fouilles de Thasos, 1921–22," *BCH* 47 (1923): Pls. 7, 8. Picard suggests that they were hidden behind the solid front of the proskenion and supported engaged columns or pilasters on the façade of the skene above. The construction appears very similar to that at Isthmia.

35. Above, p. 100.

Fig. 54. Palmette antefixes from the scene-building of the second Roman period, straight-leaf variety (IT 428, 469).

Fig. 55. Palmette antefixes from the scene-building of the second Roman period, curved-leaf type (IT 430, 435).

the other the leaves are slightly curved (Fig. 55); otherwise the pattern is virtually the same. The straight-leaved type is the most numerous, with twenty-three examples including seven whole palmettes.[36] The maximum height is 0.210 m and maximum width 0.171 m. There are five straight leaves on either side of a center leaf, the top of which is divided into three

36. IT 515, 685, 693, 428, 533, 469, 504, 418, 728, 154, 498, 444, 690, and ten uninventoried fragments. Others were placed with the pottery.

Fig. 56. Roof tiles stamped Ποσειδῶνος.

Fig. 57. Drawing of the Ποσειδῶνος stamp.

Fig. 58. Drawings of three stamps from roof tiles.

parts meeting in a point; all rise from an oval heart on a stem flanked by spirals. At the edges a small spiral on a stem curves inward. The bottom edge is divided into two bands. A curved cover-tile was attached to the lower half, indicating that there was no sima. Whitewash was applied to the soft surface of the coarse clay, only on the front of the antefix. Inasmuch as all examples are identical, they seem to have come from the same mold or family of molds. The inferior quality of workmanship makes it probable that they were locally made, perhaps in a factory near the sanctuary.

The type with curved leaves is represented by sixteen examples including two complete palmettes.[37] Their maximum height is 0.185 m and width 0.192 m, which gives them a more nearly square outline than the others. The design varies only in having curved leaves and vertical relief lines between the bands at the bottom; the execution is even more cursory. The fragments of both types were found mixed together, and they undoubtedly came from the same roof where one type may have been made for later repairs.

A large number of stamped roof tiles also came to light in the theater. They are all large curved pan tiles of the Roman type, stamped on the top near the center. No complete example has been recovered to provide the dimensions of the tile. The clay is brick-red like that of the antefixes, with a soft, buff surface. The tiles are 0.021 m to 0.028 m thick; the stamps are generally located 0.16 m to 0.20 m from an edge. The types represented include the name Ποσειδῶνος (Figs. 56, 57), a dolphin with a trident placed diagonally behind (Fig. 58, no. 1), the name ΒΑΛΕΡΙ and the dolphin and trident design done in raised outline on the right side (Fig. 58, no. 2), and the words ΕΠΙ ΑΡ ΖΕΝ (Fig. 58, no. 3) with a small dolphin between ΑΡ and ΖΕΝ. The stamped tiles will be discussed by M. Jameson and D. Geagan in their forthcoming publications of the inscriptions from Isthmia. Only the tiles bearing the stamp Ποσειδῶνος were found in sufficient quantities around the skene and orchestra to warrant the conclusion that they came from the roof of the scene-building. The letter forms resemble those in a victor list found near the Palaimonion[38] and those on a statue base in the sanctuary labeled "Juventianus, priest." This is undoubtedly the benefactor of Isthmia whose career fell during the reign of Antoninus Pius or Marcus Aurelius.[39] An even closer parallel to the letters is found

37. IT 417, 419, 725, 434, 514, 684, 435, 429, and eight uninventoried fragments.

38. Broneer, *Hesperia* 28 (1959): 324, Pl. 65b.

39. Ibid., 27 (1958): 23, Pl. 9d, and especially n. 23 where Broneer discusses the problem of chronology. See Kent, *Inscriptions*, p. 89, no. 201, and nos. 199, 200, and 306, which contain references to Juventianus and are dated between the middle of the second century and A.D. 170.

on an ephebic list containing the name of Marcus Aurelius, found in 1963 on Paros.[40]

The Parodoi

Although the parodoi were never rearranged to run parallel to the scene-building, vaults were added across their upper half to join the cavea to the wings of the skene. According to the usual Roman theater design, the cavea and scene-building formed a single unit with vaulted parodoi beneath the sides of the cavea.[41] Such a plan was carried out at Corinth where the romanization was more complete and the parodoi were totally rebuilt and reoriented.[42]

Remains of the vault and its supporting walls are especially plentiful in the west parodos. Heavy walls were constructed along each side with a clear space of 3.50 m to 3.70 m between them. The north wall, which replaced its predecessor from the second Greek period, is about 1.10 m thick and is preserved to a height of 1.80 m. The type of masonry used here and in the corresponding wall on the south side is peculiar (Fig. 59, 60), and it is found only in the theater in the second Roman period[43] and in a recently discovered structure built into the trans-Isthmian fortification north of the theater. The first course is composed of large, well-cut rectangular blocks resting on a bedding of lime mortar, and the upper part has a rubble concrete core faced with small stones. Each stone is cut with only one rectangular face, about 0.22 m by 0.14 m on the average, and they are laid in courses with a large quantity of mortar. The west end of the wall is finished with a large block in the upper portion also, and there is another large block at the east end of the preserved section. The south wall is also 1.10 m thick and preserved to a height of 1.42 m; it was placed against the analemma of the first Roman period (Figs. 18, 59). At the east end there is a cement bedding for a large block projecting about 0.35 m into the parodos, which probably marked the eastern limit of the vault. The eastern extension of the parodoi walls has been destroyed except for the cement bedding.

If the vault began at the block projecting on the south side, it would have

40. G. Daux, "Chronique des Fouilles et Découvertes archéologiques en Grèce en 1963," *BCH* 88 (1964): 808–9, 813, Fig. 2.

41. Bieber, *Greek and Roman Theater*, p. 187.

42. See Stillwell, *Theatre*, pp. 49–58, Pl. VIIa. At Babylon, Syracuse, and Pompeii the parodoi were also rebuilt parallel to the skene in the Roman period. Dinsmoor points out that at Ephesos, Termessos, and Side they were vaulted but retained their former orientation (*AAG*, p. 319).

43. This construction appears in terrace walls c-c and d-d and in the storeroom as well as in the parodoi.

Fig. 59. South wall of the west parodos, looking southwest. Note two fragments from Doric columns in center.

Fig. 60. North wall of the west parodos (a-a), looking north.

been opposite the sixth row of the cavea, 1.88 m above the orchestra.[44] The height of the vault above its supporting walls would have been about 1.80 m (equal to one-half the width of the parodos) and its arch would have been about 180°; the entire opening from ground to apex would have been about 3.60 m and its width 3.60 m. Above the vault there may have been a *tribunalium* where seats of honor were provided for special guests.[45]

On the east side of the theater where the destruction was more complete nothing is left except the footing trench for the north wall (b-b, Pl. I), 0.87 m thick, and ten blocks from the first course of the south wall. A slight setback for the upper courses of the south wall is indicated by a setting line and weathering along the inside edge. The blocks from the earlier analemma have also been removed with the exception of two near the west end, but the analemma was in place when the new parodos wall was built. From the number of small stones with one rectangular face found in the debris we may conclude that the upper part of the walls was of the same construction as the walls on the west side.

At a point just inside the lower end of the vaults, in the south walls of both parodoi, the blocks of the first course project slightly from the outer face. On the east side the total length of the projecting portion is 2.06 m and the width of projection is 0.48 m; on the west it is 1.83 m long and 0.37 to 0.44 m wide. The top surfaces of both the projections have been cut down as if to remove them from view. This, coupled with the absence of a similar projection on the north side, leads to the suggestion that some feature was planned for the parodoi, but the plan was changed before the foundations were laid for the north walls. Afterward the projecting surfaces were cut down.

In the upper part of the west parodos were found two large Doric column fragments, each broken at one end but without a join. Patches of stucco cling to the flutes. Fragment I, lying farther to the west (on the right side in Fig. 59), has sixteen flutes and a diameter on the preserved end of 0.53 m, taken on the arris, and on the broken end 0.51 m. Near the intact end is an unfluted section 0.35 m high and at least three flutes wide, and on the opposite side of the drum there is a long narrow cutting (0.14 m long, beginning 0.40 m from the end) to hold perhaps a grill or grating. The other fragment (II), lying farther east, has a diameter of 0.50 m at the finished end and 0.51 m at the broken one. Here, too, there is an unfluted section near the preserved end, 0.51 m high and the same width as the

44. Vitruvius specifies that one-sixth the diameter of the orchestra should determine the amount of the cavea to be cut back for the vault (v. 6. 5). At Isthmia this would be one-sixth of 17.40 m or 2.90 m, 0.60 m short of the actual amount. See the theaters at Fiesole (Bieber, *Greek and Roman Theater*, p. 194, Figs. 655–57), Pompeii (ibid., p. 173, Figs. 606, 611), and Syracuse (Rizzo, *Syracuse*, Figs. 26, 27).

45. See Bieber, *Greek and Roman Theater*, p. 187, and the theaters mentioned in n. 44.

other. Because of the similarity in material, dimensions, and workmanship of the two fragments, they probably belonged to the same column or pair of columns. Fragment I is 1.07 m high, fragment II is 1.25 m. If fragment I is taken as coming from the bottom of the shaft with a lower diameter of 0.53 m and the height was seven times the diameter,[46] the column, including capital, would have been about 3.71 m high. This is close to the height of the vaulted entrances to the parodoi, and the columns may have stood as decorations on either side of the opening. Then the unfluted sections would have stood against the projecting moldings on the parodos walls.

The Court

In the Greek and early Roman periods there appear to have been no permanent constructions north of the scene-building where the natural ground level was about 1.20 m above the orchestra and declined gradually to the north. The early Roman sherds in the fill point to the fact that additional earth was brought in to level off the area in the first century of our era. Finally, in the second period the space was utilized for a large court that greatly expanded the theater complex. The irregular shape of the court seems to have resulted from its having been laid out in relation to existing structures (see chap. 3, p. 75). Both the east and west walls continue the line of the ends of the skene and the south wall follows the orientation of the wings except for a short segment in the center at right angles to the central passage (Fig. 41). The north wall runs almost due east and west according to the compass[47] and thus corresponds to the orientation of the main temple and sanctuary. Although little else is known of them, other buildings adjacent to the theater on the north and west had the same alignment (see below, pp. 116 ff., 126 ff.). The entire court has a maximum exterior length of 36.50 m and a width of 18.70 m.

The east, west, and south walls are well enough preserved to give some idea of their construction. Large rectangular blocks, many of which bear signs of former use, are bedded on a foundation of concrete that varies in depth according to the level of the hardpan. The joints between the blocks are tight, without mortar, and no clamps are evident. A few patches of mortar are preserved on the top surface of the west wall, and cracks at various intervals are filled with mortar. In the first course only the interior face is evenly finished, and the blocks protrude irregularly on the outside. In the south wall the first course is intact for three-quarters of its length, and the second is in place at the western end (Pl. I). At the east end the

---

46. See chap. 3, n. 34, regarding the proportions of Doric columns in the Roman period.
47. It will be remembered that, according to the compass, the theater is oriented slightly north by northeast.

blocks rested almost directly on the clay, but where the wall crossed the central drain a cement foundation, 0.70 m thick and supporting an additional course of blocks, lies below the first course. The silt that filled the early stream bed through the center of the theater apparently made the heavier foundation necessary at this point. The first course of the south wall is 0.33 m high, but the blocks vary greatly in length and to some extent also in width. The second course has a height of 0.45 m and a thickness of about 0.67 m. In view of the unevenness of the exterior face, the ground level outside the court must have reached at least to the top of the second course (+ 1.28 m) and probably above.

On the interior the blocks of the second course are smoothly finished and set in 0.07 m from the line of the first course, which forms the euthynteria. All the blocks in the second course of the south wall appear to have come from a Doric epistyle (see chap. 3, pp. 77–80). On the two blocks lying face upward the projecting taenias and triglyphs have been almost completely cut away to prepare a smooth bedding for a third course. It is evident that the court walls rose to at least three courses and probably continued to a height of 2 to 3 m.[48]

The two courses of the west wall correspond in character and dimensions to those in the south wall. The east wall stands to a height of only one course for over half its length; at the north end the blocks are missing, and the cement foundations mark its course. Mortar was used on the top of the blocks presumably as a bedding for the next course.

In the north wall no blocks are preserved. Here a heavy cement bedding was laid against the foundation for another wall to the north of it (Pl. I). This northern wall and the structure to which it belonged will be discussed below (pp. 116–19) together with the blocks marked f and 3 and others in the series of tie blocks that extend through the court wall. On the west side the concrete foundation of the court wall continued at least across the entrance road, and on the east it went beyond the road and into the unexcavated area where it seems to have formed the north wall of the second northeast building. The cement foundation presumably carried a wall of rectangular blocks like the other three walls of the court.

Although no hard-packed earthen floor could be distinguished anywhere over the entire surface of the court, nor is there any evidence of a more permanent pavement, a layer of white clay about 0.20 m thick did appear at a number of places and probably represents the floor. It is most conspicuous around the center and north side of the court where it lies at a level of + 0.53 m to + 0.60 m. At the north it was clearly interrupted by the removal of the blocks from the wall and thus predates the destruction.

48. Cf. the construction of the court behind the theater at Corinth (Stillwell, *Theatre*, pp. 64–65, Fig. 57).

The level of the clay *strosis* rises to about +1.08 m along the west wall, perhaps because of a late colonnade that was erected there (see below, p. 116). It must also have been as high along the east side in order to have covered the northwest drain, the sides of which now reach to +0.74 m without cover slabs. The drain descends as it proceeds toward the center of the court until the sides are at a level of only +0.11 m where they join the central drain. A coin of Commodus (A.D. 176–192, IC 707) was found at the east side of the court at about +1.10 m, which was approximately the floor level. Along the south wall the setback of the second course (+0.83 m) would have been a little above the floor, and a *strosis* a little below that (+0.73 m to +0.63 m) probably represents the level of use in the court. Thus, the floor was slightly lower in the center and sloped down to its lowest point, +0.53 m, in the middle of the north side, very likely to facilitate drainage.

Nowhere are there any foundations that could have belonged to an interior colonnade, which is so often found in connection with theaters and is especially recommended by Vitruvius (v. 9. 1).[49] At Corinth the court behind the scene-building, irregular in shape as at Isthmia, was finished inside with a colonnaded walk on all four sides.[50] The odeum just south of the theater also had an irregular court with a colonnade on three sides.[51] The absence of interior colonnades at Isthmia may be a result of the generally unfinished state of the theater. In any case, the court was apparently left as an open peribolos surrounded by a wall 2–3 m high. To provide shade or shelter during the festival it would have been a simple matter to erect temporary awnings supported by wooden posts.

At a later time perhaps, the wall was lowered to the level of the second course, and on the top of the second course a series of rough supports was evidently erected on the south and west sides. A similar one may have continued along the east side, although all trace of it has been removed with the blocks of the second course. Six shallow cuttings, more or less rectangular, are faintly discernible on the soft stone. The first one occurs 2.27 m from the north end of the west wall and measures about 0.60 m by 0.60 m. Three more appear on the west wall with a space of 2.40 m to 2.47 m between them and measuring 0.78 m by ?, 0.68 m by 0.64 m, and 0.70 m by ? from north to south. They may have been set back 0.08 m to 0.10 m from the east face, but this is not certain. After a distance of 2.93 m, at the southwest corner, a cutting 0.70 m wide is visible on the south wall, followed by another about 2.78 m farther east, 0.69 m wide.

49. Vitruvius mentions colonnades as being attached to the theater of Pompey at Rome (Bieber, *Greek and Roman Theater*, pp. 181–82, Figs. 630, 632, for a reconstruction), to the theater of Dionysos at Athens (in the form of the Stoa of Eumenes), and to other theaters.
50. Stillwell, *Theatre*, pp. 64 ff., Pl. VII.
51. Broneer, *The Odeum*, pp. 67 ff., Fig. 45.

Here the second course is interrupted, and presumably the series continued the length of the wall. Because of the approximate regularity of the cuttings it is possible that they served as beddings for a series of supports, probably of wood. The clay floor inside the court (at a level of +0.55 m to +0.60 m) may have been raised at this time to bring it closer to the level of the stylobate (+1.26 m). What kind of roof the supports held is not clear; it would have had to be attached to the terrace wall c-c (and d-d, if the supports continued also on the east side) and to the rear wall of the scene-building. If such an arrangement did indeed surround the court at one time, it would have taken the place of colonnades on the inside. Although of such a rude style, it is not impossible that these colonnades were substituted at the time construction in the theater was suspended.

One entrance to the court would have been located in the south wall opposite the central passage where a stretch of the south wall runs at right angles to the passage. Although the greater part of this section of the wall lies west of the axis, the line of the axis is roughly marked on the top of the first course and it may be assumed that an entrance would have been centered on the passage and skene. Therefore, the distance of 0.68 m between the axis and the east end of this stretch of wall may be taken as one-half the width of the entrance; the total would have been 1.36 m. Beyond this nothing else remains.

A small rectangular basin with inside dimensions of 1.15 m by 0.92 m is located just outside the northeast corner of the court (Pl. I). Only the foundations of concrete are preserved, but it seems to have been a small drinking fountain, perhaps for the spectators and their animals. A terracotta pipe lying just below the surface of the eastern entrance road may have been its source of supply, bringing water from some place southwest of the theater.[52]

The "Stoa"

North of the court there are two long parallel foundations, the southern one of which, contiguous with the north wall of the court, has been exposed for a considerable distance. The northern one has been followed in small trenches at points 4 and 5 on Plate I and at other places along its course. Trenches were opened in an attempt to uncover a western cross wall connecting the two long walls, but no trace of one was found and the north wall comes to an ill-defined end without a return. At the east end both foundations continue beyond the excavated area. If these foundations were intended for a building, the absence of a west end wall may indicate that it never progressed beyond the early stages of construction. Such a long narrow structure adjacent to the theater would have been suit-

52. All nine water pipes that enter the theater area come from a southwesterly direction.

able for a stoa, but too little even of the foundations has been uncovered to reach a conclusion on this point.

The south foundation, 0.92 m thick, is bordered by the north wall of the court, which is identical in its composition and texture of rubble concrete. They were not, however, laid as one homogeneous mass. Both faces of the north foundation are lined with small stones that are slightly larger than those used in the concrete and seem to have been intended for outside facing. The court wall, poured against it, lacks this facing. Also, the north foundation was laid considerably deeper than that of the court, perhaps because it was supposed to carry a heavier wall. In the first test trench west of the axis the north foundation reached about 0.85 m deeper than the court wall and about 1.55 m below the floor of the court. At block 3 (Pl. I) it extended to the bottom of the early theater drain (about −2.73 m) while the court foundation stopped at −0.69 m.

At regular intervals of approximately 6 m, large rectangular blocks were set into the south foundation of the "stoa" with a portion projecting from the south face. Three of the blocks are in place and the foundation block for one more together with the holes left by two others have been found. Block f is the westernmost of those remaining, followed by block 3 to the east, and the final block stands at the north side of the northeast building. There were very likely others along the wall because they are nearly evenly spaced. Block f is of well-cut poros stone, finished on the south, east, and west sides and rebated at the point where it protruded from the wall (Fig. 61). It rests on two blocks, one in the wall and the other in the court side. It is 1.63 m wide and 0.62 m long on the south side, 0.675 m long on the north, and it is 0.97 m high. The projecting portion is evenly cut on all sides. Block 3 is very similar to f. The easternmost block is different in that it lacks the rebate; it is 1.40 m wide by 0.67 m long, and the top has been damaged by a plow.

In view of the fact that the "stoa" foundation was laid first, the tie blocks would have been part of the original construction and were perhaps intended to serve as buttresses.[53] Since one of the blocks was located in the center of the eastern entrance road, that building appears to have been begun before the court and roads were planned in their present form. This is further confirmed by the ground level outside of the proposed structure, which was about −0.28 m to −0.31 m, or about 0.81 m below the floor of the court at the north side, inasmuch as the tie blocks were finished down to that level and were evidently supposed to be seen. It may be that work on the "stoa" was interrupted by the expansion of the theater complex and never resumed.

53. Cf. the peribolos behind the theater at Corinth, which had exterior buttresses (Stillwell, *Theatre*, p. 65, Pl. II), and the early Roman temenos wall in the Sanctuary of Poseidon at Isthmia.

Fig. 61. Opening for the central drain to pass through the "stoa" wall, looking north. Note block f and the block added to the west side of the central drain at the juncture with northwest drain (arrow).

Fig. 62. Marble epistyle block (IA 1999), top surface in foreground.

At the northeast end of the excavated area a marble epistyle block (IA 1999) was found at a low level just south of the south "stoa" wall. The white marble block, broken at one end, is preserved to a length of 1.80 m, and it is 0.49 m wide by 0.505 m high (Fig. 62). On the bottom runs a recessed, curved molding that stretched between the supports. The clear span between the supports would have been about 1.32 m and the total length of the block 1.94 m. The order is Ionic (or Corinthian) with the architrave and frieze cut in the same block. The one broad and one narrow fascia are smoothly finished, but the other moldings are merely blocked in and the surface of the architrave was left rough. On the top of the block in the center is a square dowel hole. In the earth over the block, fragments of an abacus from a white marble Corinthian capital and a small piece from one of the leaves came to light. The workmanship on both is very fine, and their proportions are right for a capital belonging to the marble epistyle block. What building these were intended for it is impossible to say; the block does have an unfinished appearance.

The Central Drain

Since the greater part of the drain was constructed in its present form during the first Roman period (chap. 3, pp. 80–82), only the section that was rebuilt in connection with the north wall of the court and "stoa" will be treated here.

Where the channel was crossed by the "stoa" foundations at the level of the first course (the course below block f), a large rectangular block (0.48 m high), inserted into the foundations below this level, formed the channel floor (Fig. 61).[54] The channel itself, 0.68 m high and 0.90 m wide, passes through the first course and is covered by a large rectangular block in the second course. The joints inside are tight, and there is no trace of a stucco lining. The cover block that is included in the "stoa" wall has a large arched mouth cut into its south face, 0.84 m wide and 0.68 m high, sloping down into the channel (Fig. 61). The upper section of the mouth, which would have been cut through the court wall, is missing, but from the angle of the remaining portion we can estimate that the original top of the mouth in the south face of the court wall would have been above the level of the court floor. This opening was very likely planned to receive rainwater from the court floor that in turn was sloped to channel it in this direction. A normal man-hole inlet in the floor at the rear of the court would not explain the presence of the arch-shaped block between the court and "stoa" walls.

54. The floor of the channel at this point is 0.30 m above the original bottom of the central drain (chap. 3, p. 82). Since it is unlikely that the water in the drain would have been allowed to back up at this change in level, the old channel probably had been filled up with silt to that level when the new channel opening was made.

An amphora, broken but almost complete, was found just south of the junction between the northwest drain and central drain below the floor level. It appears to have been dropped in the artificial fill brought to even out the ground when the court was built, and it is very similar to the amphora built into the later stair at the end of the central passage (see above, p. 103, Fig. 53).

A drain coming from the southeast entered the theater area a few meters from the storeroom and continued northwest to empty into the central drain (Pl. I, Fig. 61). The sides of the drain are carefully made with bricks laid horizontally in mortar, and the floor is paved with pan tiles. The cover slabs of poros are intact over a stretch to the southeast and also under the entrance road. They are evenly cut and tightly joined in keeping with the careful construction exhibited by the drain as a whole. Where it enters the theater area it is 0.43 m wide and 0.33 m deep. After a distance of 7.50 m it led into an almost cubical clearing basin, 0.86 m square, which is made in the same fashion as the drain (Fig. 63). From the basin the channel passed under the entrance road where it narrowed to 0.35 m and deepened to 0.45 m. A passage for the drain was cut through the first course of the court wall; it then ran across the court at an angle and joined the central drain 1.55 m from the north wall. At the point of juncture the sides of the central drain were raised 0.70 m to compensate for the difference in height between the two (Fig. 61).

Fig. 63. Clearing basin in the northwest drain, looking east.

The northwest drain is obviously later than the central drain, but the date of its construction is not known. It is also later than wall d-d that would have been in place when the clearing basin was placed against it. The earth inside the bottom of the basin contained sherds from the second half of the second century A.D., and the latest pottery in the upper part and inside the drain belongs to the late third and early fourth centuries, by which time the water system would have ceased to function.

The Entrance Roads

The open approaches from the east and west sides were blocked by two long walls, c-c on the west and d-d on the east side (Pl. I). Along the walls new entrances were arranged by means of roads leading into the theater from the north, between the walls and the court. Both roads are about 4.50 m wide; the eastern one reaches to 33.40 m in length while the one on the west stops at 28.80 m, the difference being due to the diagonal orientation of the north wall of the court. Because the ground on the west side sloped down to the north, the surface of the road had to be artificially raised with fill composed of soft clay and poros chips, devoid of any pottery (Fig. 42). There was no evidence of road metal on the surface of the western road; on the east side there was a hard, smooth layer built up by heavy foot traffic over a long period of time (Fig. 64). Evidently the majority of spectators entered the theater from the northeast, and it is

Fig. 64. East entrance road, looking south. Arrow at left marks clearing basin.

questionable whether the western entrance was ever open at all. The pottery that accumulated over the east road indicates that it continued to be used to the mid-fifth century, almost one hundred and seventy-five years after the theater had ceased to function.

Another road between the skene and the court was used by people to cross from one side to the other, and at the junction with the west road a trodden surface is evident, continuing southward to the parodos. The spectators must have entered on the east and used this road to reach their seats on the west side (Fig. 41). The surface is preserved at a level of + 1.19 m. The road was obviously not blocked by the court entrance at the end of the central passage.

The terrace walls c-c and d-d are 27.65 m and 33.95 m long, respectively (Pl. I). On the west the ground rises to a height of 1.18 m to 1.32 m above the road; on the east the difference is only about 0.43 m. Probably because the ground behind c-c was higher, it is the heavier of the two walls, with a thickness of 0.67 m as compared to 0.58 m for d-d. Both walls were constructed very much like the parodos walls as far as may be ascertained from a short section preserved to a height of 0.60 m at the south end of d-d. The foundation blocks continue northward for another 8.80 m, but beyond that only the cement bedding is left together with cuttings that show that the wall was stepped down at intervals following the slope of the land. In c-c the foundation blocks appear at the south end, and the bedding extends for the rest of the wall. Bits of mortar and stones were found clinging to the clay scarp where they had filled in the space between the wall and the clay.

The long walls are nearly parallel to the sides of the court, and from the fact that they share the construction technique of the parodos walls it is evident that they belong to the second Roman period of reconstruction.

The West Terraces

The ground on the west side that rose rather steeply has been leveled off into two terraces. The eastern one lies along wall c-c that served as its retaining wall; on the west it was bounded by wall e-e that retained the second terrace above (Pl. I). The eastern terrace thus delimited was 3.40 m wide and 27.50 m long, from the cavea to an extension of the south "stoa" wall. The clay at the south end was covered with a thin layer of macadam that may have been the pavement. Near the center on the east edge lies a cement foundation 2.65 m long and set 0.25 m into the clay scarp. The horizontal grooves on its surface were very likely made by step blocks belonging to a stairway leading up from the west road.

The north end of the two west terraces is crossed by a number of walls and water channels at different levels, all in such a poor state of preservation that any restoration is impossible without further investigation to the west where more remains of the same complex protrude above ground.

At the time of the second Roman period, the terrace wall e-e (0.81 m thick) may have extended as far as the end of c-c, where a limestone block (0.80 m by 0.83 m and lying 3.50 m west of the block at the north end of c-c) would have marked its northern terminus (Pl. I). Apparently at a later time the northern half of e-e was removed and a heavy east-west wall (about 1.10 m thick) was laid out. Because it was oriented with the north wall of the court and the "stoa," it forms an acute angle with c-c. Only the cement bedding is left of this wall, 0.92 m below e-e and 7.15 m south of the line of the "stoa" south wall. From the beginning the continuation of the intended rear (south) wall of the "stoa" may have formed a boundary line for the area and determined its orientation. The heavy wall began at c-c and ran westward for 12.40 m to a point where it formed two steps (see the analemmata and wall d-d) and continued at a level about 1.35 m higher and with a smaller width of 0.65 m (Fig. 65). A section of its northern face is exposed some meters west of the excavated area for an additional 15.30 m, which indicates a structure of considerable size.

Another even heavier cement foundation (1.74 m thick) at the lower level abuts the south wall at right angles to it and 4.30 m west of c-c (Pl. I). The wall ran northward for 7.80 m and then seems to have turned westward. The deep fill of broken clay, white earth, pebbles, and poros chips that covers the area also continues over this foundation, and it appears that the wall was removed during the use of the building.

The northern limits of the resulting enclosure (marked VI on Pl. I) are not so clearly defined because the thin layer of top soil did not protect it from the plow. Some traces of a continuation of the south wall of the "stoa" are evident at a level about 0.80 m above the two beddings described above, but its connection with the north-south wall is not clear. In any case the water channel, explained below, would have been precisely contiguous with the south face of the "stoa" wall extension.

Two small sections of a rough mosaic floor with large white tesserae were uncovered *in situ* inside the south wall, together with the cement bedding for larger portions.[55] An even greater piece of the floor lies on its side at the far east end where it slipped into the plundered trench of wall c-c (Fig. 66), and another fell into the trench of the south wall, also at the east end. The floor is at a level of about 1.06 m above the entrance road, and it seems likely that the entire enclosure was paved with the mosaic, fragments of which were found scattered about the area. Because the eastern section of the floor lies directly in the line of e-e, it would have been laid after the removal of the wall if it did indeed extend that far north.

55. Pieces of a similar mosaic were found in the later stadium, but not *in situ*.

Fig. 65. West terrace; south water channel and south wall of enclosure, looking northwest.

Fig. 66. Rough mosaic floor fallen from the enclosure at the north end of the west terrace, looking west. West entrance road with pipes in foreground.

The entire area was liberally supplied with water from a pair of channels that entered from the west (Pl. I). One runs along the north side and the other along the south side of the enclosure (VI, Pl. I) in close connection with the walls. The southern channel is in much the better state of preservation with well-constructed sides (0.49 m wide) made of triangular bricks laid in mortar (see the northwest drain and clearing basin). They rise to their original height of 1.12 m, and marks of the cover slabs are visible along the edges (Fig. 66). The sides and cement floor are broken off after a distance of 6 m but a bedding continues for another 2.35 m. Since the intact portion of the channel corresponds with the upper section of the south wall, it may be supposed that its eastern extension was connected with the lower part of the wall and was hence destroyed by the removal of the wall. A coin of the emperor Gallienus (A.D. 253–268) came to light in the bottom of the channel. A basin made with rubble cement and lined with watertight stucco and a tile floor (0.88 m by 1.00 m on the inside) is located at the south side of the south wall. It is probably related to the waterworks of the enclosure, although the connection has been lost with the loss of the top portion. Faint traces of perhaps another wall foundation, 0.55 m wide, appear on the cement bedding at the west end of the channel on the north side, but the plow has removed any further evidence of the wall.

The northern channel, 0.51 m wide, would have resembled the southern one, but it is in a very ruined state. Most of it is gone except for one course of bricks along the south side and a few from the north at the east end (Pl. I). The cement floor is lacking here, and the sides appear to rest on loose fill at a higher level than on the south side. The channel runs eastward for 13.20 m and then stops; perhaps at this point it made a turn to the south.

In summary, the eastern section of an enclosure with an overall width of about 9 m has been uncovered at the north end of the west terrace. The floor was covered with a rough white mosaic, and two water channels followed the north and south walls well into the area. Originally a cross wall may have limited the eastern end of the enclosure about 5 m from the terrace wall c-c, but later that section was also covered by the mosaic floor. The enclosure is part of a larger structure lying to the west of the excavated area and not closely connected to the theater. More cannot be hazarded until the remainder of the building is laid bare.

A number of terra-cotta pipes entered the theater area from the southwest, i.e., from the direction of the main temenos and the reservoirs nearby.[56] They will be described beginning with the southernmost pipe (1) and proceeding northward in numerical order except for pipe (9) (Pl. I). All the pipes are of Roman manufacture. They have a maximum outer diameter of about 0.12–15 m and are composed of sections 0.35–0.52 m long, carefully fitted together with hard, waterproof stucco. The clay is for the most part of the yellow-white variety native to Corinthia, but some of the pipes are also made from reddish clay. None of them can be followed to its destination, and, with one exception, they appear to have supplied waterworks outside the theater.

Pipe (1) enters the theater along the outside of the first cavea pier on the west end (Pl. I), and further on a small section is visible at the west end of the analemma. Beyond that to the east and north there are two sections of pipe (2) and (3) that may have been connected to pipe (1). Beginning at e-e, pipe (2) runs parallel to the analemma to the edge of the terrace where it drops down to the road. A terra-cotta elbow joint that was found at the point of the drop was very likely part of this pipe. After turning north and running along c-c for some distance, pipe (2) is broken off at the stairway to the west terrace. A section that appears again at the north end of the road and running in the same direction is probably a continuation of (2). Pipe (3) consists of a short section embedded in the surface of the terrace west of e-e and in the foundation of e-e. It is in the same line with pipe (1) and may have been part of (1) until (2) replaced it. In any case, pipes (2),

56. See the northwest reservoir (Broneer, *Hesperia* 31 [1962]: 14) and a later Roman reservoir system that has not been fully explored or published, but that ran under the north side of the temenos and eastward under the theater cave. Manholes in the northeast section of the temenos and in the east chamber of the cave have been cleared.

(3), (4), and (5) were in place when e-e was poured; they are surrounded by the cement. Pipe (9) may be earlier since it is buried in a trench 0.40 m wide and 1.05 m deep, which passes well under e-e. Although (9) was uncovered for a distance of only 2.50 m, it continued in a northeast direction until it was interrupted by c-c. A section of the pipe protrudes from the scarp to mark the point of the break. Pipe (4) passes through e-e north of (9) and parallel to (3). Pipe (5) has a more westerly orientation and has been uncovered from a point near the western edge of the excavated area, through e-e, and up to the edge of the scarp. It appears to have been cut off by the stair at its east end. Another pipe (6) lies very close to (5) but at a level about 0.30–0.40 m above it. From the way in which the cement of e-e has been cut away to provide passage for the pipe, it seems to postdate the wall. East of e-e the pipe swerves northward to avoid the stair and then descends rapidly as it crosses the terrace. It is the largest of all the pipes and may have been connected to a pipe at the north end of the road (Fig. 41). Pipe (6) probably replaced (5) when the terraces were constructed.

Pipe (7) begins in the center of the west entrance road and runs eastward along the south wall of the court. There is no sign of it farther east, although it may well have joined pipe (8), which appears in the east road. Pipe (8) was broken off near the north end of the road where the whole surface has been disturbed by the plow, but it could have supplied water to the rectangular basin nearby.

The Eastern Area

The space east of long wall d-d contained two permanent buildings and perhaps some temporary ones at this time. At the south end the storeroom was built about 6.80 m from the unfinished cavea (Pl. I, Fig. 67). Its name comes from the fact that it may have been used originally for storing equipment and scenery for the theater.[57] Later it was enlarged and, finally, after the theater was deserted, it continued to be used for some unknown purpose.

As it was first constructed, the storeroom had an interior space of 4.55 m by 6.05 m and was closed on the west by a portion of wall d-d. The north and south walls, which are partially preserved, exhibit the same type of construction as found in the parodoi walls. On the east the wall has been almost completely obliterated except for traces of the cement bedding.

Pieces of fallen masonry were found scattered about inside and outside the room in a concentration not seen elsewhere on the east side. Much of it apparently came from the upper parts of the building where the walls

57. Small rooms on this order are found in Roman theaters built into the rear of the scene-building; e.g., the theaters at Arles and Orange (Formigé, *Remarques*, pp. 56–57, Pl. I, Fig. 1). Vitruvius (v. 9. 8) mentions that they were used also as general storage depots.

were made of square bricks laid in mortar of a thickness equal to that of the bricks. Some sections of masonry showing a slight curve indicate that the room was covered by a brick vault with the bricks set vertically. Many of the individual bricks have two curved ends, one concave and the other convex, with sides converging slightly toward the concave end.

Inside the room three hard-packed earthen floors are distinguishable. The first (lowest) is easily separated from the second over the entire area of the room; the second and third are not so clearly defined. The first, belonging to the original building, lay at approximately the same level as the east road (+1.19 m) but about 0.43 m below ground level outside to the north.[58] Next to the north wall many thin pieces of glass were un-

58. The outside (north) face of the northwest corner block is finished only at the top in a band 0.10 m wide. The outside ground level would have been about +1.62 m or 0.10 m below the top of the block. This level agrees with the remainder of the wall surface, which is very rough and uneven and would have been below ground level.

Fig. 67. The storeroom, looking east. Note roof tiles stacked in lower right corner.

covered where they had fallen, apparently from a window in the north wall about 2.60 m from the west end. Patches of white stucco adhering to the lower part of the west wall are the remains of the interior finish.

At a later time the east wall of the room was moved eastward beyond the excavated area, so that it is not possible to determine the extent of the enlargement. The north and south walls also were consequently extended but in a slightly different style of masonry. The second earthen floor, lying about 0.15 m above the first, spread across the foundation for the original east wall and so may be associated with the enlargement of the room.

Whatever its original purpose, it was used as a storeroom in the second period. Two rows of forty to fifty roof tiles came to light neatly stacked on the second floor level in the southwest corner, and more tiles are scattered nearby, as if they had been stacked also, farther north (Fig. 67). The stacked tiles are all of the curved variety, though pan tiles were found in the vicinity; the room seems to have been a depository for roofing materials. In the northwest corner a fire left a dense deposit of carbon dust over about one-quarter of the room. The inside face of the walls show the effects of intense heat.

The third or uppermost floor level inside the room seems not to have extended to the west wall but to have been confined to the eastern section, 0.33 m above the second floor. It appears to have been largely a layer of earth that accumulated after the theater went out of use. Seemingly contemporary with this floor is a poorly built wall on the east side of the original eastern wall (Pl. I). A second small wall, very uneven, projects into the room at a slightly acute angle to the east wall. The masonry includes a wide assortment of materials, many reused blocks, a poros column drum, bricks, terra-cotta roof tiles, and marble fragments, all set in crumbly mortar. The two walls appear to be of the same period, and the east wall may have been added as a partition to divide the room. The spur wall ends in two half-columns set with their flat sides facing each other about 0.225 m apart (Fig. 67). In both columns a vertical groove has been cut into the flat side. The northern column is bluish marble rising about 0.85 m above third-floor level; it has been sawed off on both sides as well as through the middle, and thus its original diameter of about 0.36 m was reduced to 0.31 m. The groove, curved in section is 0.14 m wide and 0.045 m deep and shows no sign of wear. The southern column, which is poros, is 0.29 m in diameter and stands about 0.50 m above the floor. The groove here is more roughly cut, 0.06 m wide and 0.03 m deep, and is not placed in the center. This odd arrangement may have been connected with a waterworks, for the diagonal wall carried a channel on its top, traces of which can be discerned in the crumbly masonry. The grooves would have accommodated a sluicegate, perhaps, but it is impossible to reach any conclusions about such fragmentary remains.

In the surface of the third earthen floor two flat tiles are embedded, one next to the south wall near the later cross wall, the other near the center of the room at the edge of the third floor (Pl. I). The first tile is 0.25 m by 0.35 m, the second 0.25 m by 0.54 m. A low edge appears on three sides of each tile so that they could have been used to mix small quantities of material. An amphora, probably not later than the third century A.D., was discovered almost intact next to the south wall (Fig. 67). Also, a small poros altar or statue base, 0.46 m square with a triangular molding around the top, was found lying nearby. From its tilted position it does not seem to have belonged there and may have found its way in after the destruction.

South of the storeroom is a small area enclosed on the east side by a thin wall made of stone slabs set on edge. Inasmuch as the wall overlaps the joint where the extension of the south wall was added to the storeroom, it would have been erected after the room was enlarged. There is no indication of a south wall for the area along the cavea, so that it probably remained open to the sky. At the time of excavation the enclosure was filled with a large number of roof tiles, laid one on top of another, many bearing the stamp of a dolphin and trident (Fig. 58) and other stamps of the sanctuary (see above, p. 109). The mixture also included a quantity of palmette antefixes exhibiting a variety of types, which would have belonged to other buildings in the vicinity.

The small north-south boundary wall that divided the area north of the storeroom in the first Roman period (see chap. 3, p. 83), seems to have been removed at the time of the second remodeling. Its place was taken by wall d-d, which formed the eastern boundary of the theater area proper. There is no way of knowing the height of d-d except that it would have been carried to the height of the storeroom and the second northeast building where it served as the west wall of both buildings. In other places it may have been no more than a low terrace wall.

The first east-west wall north of the storeroom is only 2.88 m long but 0.76 m thick, and it is composed of four large poros blocks (Pl. I). The upper part was evidently made with bricks, some fragments of which still cling to the top surface of the foundation. The wall clearly did not continue eastward at the same level because hardpan lies even with the top of the foundation block at the east end, and the line of the northwest drain would have been made to fit its direction more closely if the wall had continued.[59] There may have been temporary structures east of d-d with which the foundation was connected. Wooden stalls and booths may well

---

59. The footing trench for a north-south wall at its east end belongs to the boundary wall of the preceding period, as is shown by the fact that it was filled in at the time of the second period.

have been erected along the terrace at the time of the festival for the convenience of the merchants and their customers.[60] In the next foundation trench running east-west all the blocks have been removed, and it is not altogether clear whether it was contemporary with the spur wall or with the boundary wall of the earlier period.

The Second Northeast Building

A short distance farther north lay the northeast building (in the northeast corner of the excavated area) that appears to have been completely rebuilt on essentially the same plan as in the first period (see chap. 3, pp. 83–84). The second set of foundations is composed of rubble masonry with lime mortar but without the foundation blocks and stone facing characteristic of the parodoi and other walls in the second Roman period. The south wall, just outside that of the earlier structure, was between 1.00 m and 0.75 m thick, beginning at d-d and continuing eastward beyond the excavated area (Pls. I, VIII). The eastern limit of the building is not known. The west wall seems to have been part of d-d, and a continuation of the north wall of the court appears to have formed the north wall, though most of it is destroyed. A small interior wall, located 3.38 m from the west side, divides the building into an eastern and a western section. Another inner wall separated the eastern space into a room 4.50 m long and over 5 m wide with a narrow corridor of 1 m at the north side, which could have been for a staircase. No remains of the superstructure have been identified, nor was there any indication of the use to which the building was put.

A small drainage channel, adjacent to the south wall, runs down toward d-d where it makes a right-angled turn southward and empties into the clearing basin (Pl. I). It seems to have carried off water from the roof of the building, perhaps channeled down through a pipe. Along d-d the east side of the channel is made with roughly shaped stones set in mortar with a layer of tile fragments on the top to form a bedding for the cover slabs, two of which are in place. The west side is missing. The floor was paved with large pan tiles, and the interior opening of the channel was 0.34 m wide and 0.21 m high and covered with heavy stucco. The drain seems to postdate the wall d-d, and this may be an indication that the second northeast building was constructed some years after the major part of the theater was rebuilt.

General Chronology of the Second Roman Period

The evidence for the date of the second Roman period is largely ceramic,

---

60. Arrangements of this kind around an amphitheater are illustrated in a wall painting from Pompeii depicting the riot of A.D. 59 in the amphitheater (Bieber, *Greek and Roman Theater*, Fig. 624).

Fig. 68. Bronze coin of Antoninus Pius (enlarged).

with the addition of a few coins. One of the piers from the cavea, which had fallen, was intentionally broken up by the excavators, and the sherds that were embedded in the masonry were examined by John Hayes, together with the rest of the Roman pottery from the theater. The latest of the sherds could not be placed much before the middle of the second century A.D., which provides a *terminus post quem* for the enlargement of the cavea.

At the north end of the passage through the skene a very worn *sestertius* of Antoninus Pius (A.D. 138–161; Fig. 68) appeared a little below the floor level. It can be associated with repairs to the central drain perhaps undertaken at the time of the reconstruction. Though the date of the issue appears to be 140–43, its badly worn surface is a sign of many years in circulation. A short distance farther north a large unpainted amphora of cream-colored clay was found embedded at the east side of the stairway where it could have been inserted only at the time of construction (Fig. 53). It can be dated to the second half of the second century.[61]

An almost identical amphora was uncovered beneath the floor level of the court, just south of the juncture between the central and northwest drains. Furthermore, the sherds found along the south and west walls of the court under the clay floor can be dated in the second century, from the middle to the latter part of the century. Above the floor level the pottery that would have accumulated during the use of the court is later, beginning at the end of the second century and going through the third. A coin, apparently of Hadrian (IC 836; poorly preserved), came to light lying on

61. On the almost illegible obverse of the coin is a portrait of the emperor, Antoninus Pius, and an *Annona* scene is barely identifiable on the reverse (see H. Mattingly, *Coins of the Roman Empire in the British Museum* [Oxford: The University Press, 1940], Vol. 4, no. 1226, Pl. 28, 4–5). I am indebted to Thomas Jones for this information. For the amphora a close parallel from a well in the Athenian Agora was kindly brought to my attention by Henry Robinson. See Robinson, *Pottery of the Roman Period—Chronology,* Vol. 5 of the *Athenian Agora, Results of Excavations Conducted by the American School of Classical Studies at Athens* (Princeton: American School of Classical Studies at Athens, 1959), M-102, Pl. 23. On the basis of this, the date of the amphora and the two others identical to it would fall in the second half of the second century. The date was confirmed by John Hayes.

the cement foundation for the south court wall. Although it could have been a late intrusion after the destruction, it may have fallen there from the footing trench when the walls were removed. Other material corroborating a second-century date for the court came from the two manholes (2 and 3) that belonged to the early theater drain and are located just under the north and south walls of the court. In both places sherds from the second century were found immediately below the wall foundation.

None of this material is later than the second century, and most of it seems to fall in the second half of the century. The sherds that can be dated most closely are nearer the third quarter than later, but, inasmuch as most of the pottery is coarse ware, no more precise date is possible. The period of reconstruction may have extended over some years, but the distinctive construction technique exhibited by the parodoi walls, c-c and d-d, and the storeroom, as well as the tightly organized plan of the court and roads, are indications of a unified building project. It was an ambitious program indeed and one that had to be abandoned before completion, perhaps through lack of funds and a declining interest in the festival.[62] It is noteworthy that the theater was never converted into an arena for animal shows, as were the odeum and theater at Corinth in the third century.[63]

The visit of Pausanius to Isthmia furnishes yet another indication of date for the reconstruction. As noted at the beginning of this chapter (p. 89), Pausanius mentions that the theater and the stadium are worthy to be seen. Although this is not very descriptive, it seems reasonable to suppose that the theater in question was not the patched up structure left from the time of Nero's visit a century earlier but rather the rebuilt and expanded theater complex. Therefore, the rebuilding would have occurred before Pausanius's visit sometime between 155 and 170,[64] which agrees with the evidence of the pottery and coins.

For the succeeding phases in the theater's history the central passage in the skene provides an unbroken sequence. Above the hard earth floor of the first Roman period (-0.01 m to -0.07 m) a number of thin floor surfaces with a collective thickness of 0.05 m to 0.10 m were built up in the course of the second and third centuries. These *stroses* remain intact only along the eastern edge of the passage since every time the central drain was opened the earthen floor was disturbed. The first floor surface continuing without interruption over the drain represents the final period of normal use in the theater, at the end of which the area appears to have been abandoned and maintenance of the drainage system ceased. The floor lies at a level of about $+0.04$ m, and the earth above it contained sherds from

62. Broneer, *Klio* 39 (1961): 253–54.
63. Stillwell, *Theatre*, pp. 140–41.
64. G. Roux, *Pausanias en Corinthie (Livre 2, 1 à 15)*, (Paris: Société d' Edition "Les Belles Lettres," 1958), pp. 27–29.

the middle to the end of the third century. This layer, representing the years of declining activity, built up to a depth of 0.27 m, much greater than the use layers from the earlier periods and perhaps reflecting an increased neglect of the building.[65] In the earth over the cover slabs of the drain beneath this floor the pottery is not to be dated later than the early to middle part of the third century, and the latest material found inside the drain is also of that period. This would have accumulated during the final years of activity in the theater after the drain had been cleaned out for the last time.

Another certain indication for the end of the theater as such is the large bothros that almost completely blocked the entrance to the eastern parodos (Pl. I) and certainly postdates any performances held in the theater. The material filling the deep hole included many fragments of terra-cotta sima and antefixes and pottery from the late third to the mid-fourth century.

The Final Phases

Some casual use was apparently made of the theater during the fourth and fifth centuries. As noted above, the storeroom appears to have had a later use at the level of the third floor, although the complete stamnos found in the room at that level is probably not later than the third century. A small kiln or oven occupied the center of the east parodos under the cover of the vault that may have remained standing until the end of the fifth century; the pottery on the surface of the parodos goes into the fifth century. In the east wing of the scene-building a clay pit dug in the fifth century obliterated most of the northeast section, and the room must have been virtually destroyed. The eastern entrance road had a long life, with sherds on its lower surface as late as the first half of the fifth century.[66] Above that level an even later road entered the theater just south of the storeroom and turned north along the east road. One of the latest items recovered in the theater is a coin with the insignia of Constantinus VII (A.D. 912–959; IC 837) struck over Romanus II, found on the upper road opposite the storeroom. In the southwest corner of the court a flimsy apsidal structure resembling a sheep pen was built of small stones, about 0.30 m above the original floor level of the court. It contained pottery from the late fifth century or later.

The orchestra was very likely used for some purpose, perhaps an animal pen, in this period, as the small wall closing the west parodos bears witness. A coin of Constantius II (A.D. 355–361; IC 732) was embedded in the deep

65. At a level of about +0.31 m there was a change in the earth and another packed surface; above that the sherds go down to the end of the fourth century when the vault seems to have fallen in.

66. A coin of Valentinianus I (A.D. 364–67, IC 832) was also found on the road opposite the court.

groove that was cut in the top of the proskenion sill at the center. As soon as Theodosius (A.D. 378–395) finally closed the pagan sanctuaries, an area such as Isthmia would have become a source of building material for new constructions nearby. In the years of abandonment preceding this time, the orchestra of the theater would have filled up with silt and debris washed down from higher ground. By the time men actually came to demolish the scene-building, the columns in the orchestra, and the rest of the theater, they probably had to dig through a considerable deposit of earth. It was perhaps in this process of searching for blocks that the various packed earthen floors in the orchestra were broken up and the earth fill was disturbed down to the clay bed of the hollow. Sherds and lamps from as late as the fourth century appeared just above virgin clay, and others from the fourth and fifth centuries were found below what would have been the level of the orchestra floor in earlier times. Sherds of this date also filled the cuttings for block F, the gutter, and the east analemma.

Removal of blocks from the theater appears to have been begun on the east, the side nearest the so-called Fortress of Justinian. The major part of the demolition was probably done in connection with construction of the fortress, as the incorporation of the monumental column drums in the northeast wall bears witness. As the operation progressed, the walls were stripped to the foundations, and the workmen moved farther west. At first it had seemed necessary even to dig out the foundation blocks, but the men seem to have been surfeited with material by the time they were working on the west side and there they left most of the foundations in place. The same phenomenon occurred in the Temple of Poseidon.

5

Summary and Conclusions

The First Greek Period

On the hillside northeast of the Temple of Poseidon the first theater at Isthmia was constructed sometime in the late fifth or early fourth century B.C., probably before 390 B.C. when a fire severely damaged the main temple. A few rows of seats, facing north, were cut into the side of an artificial hollow that was scooped out near the bottom of the hill in order to increase the incline. The people who could not be accommodated in the seats would have sat or stood on the bare hillside. The clay-cut cavea was very likely three-sided with a straight center section and two shorter wings that diverged as they approached the skene. As a result, the orchestra, which was delimited by the cavea on the east, west, and south and by the scene-building on the north, was trapezoidal in shape. It lay at the bottom of the artificial hollow, below the natural level of the hill.

In the orchestra a drainage channel cut in clay ran along the edge of the east wing and into a manhole leading to an underground drain (Pls. I, IV). Presumably similar channels bordered the orchestra on the south and west sides, likewise emptying into the manhole. A small altar may have stood in the orchestra near the skene just east of center. On the north side of the artificial hollow a retaining wall would have protected the scarp from erosion. In front of this wall a narrow "proskenion" appears to have stood at orchestra level. In the center of the clay bank a north-south passage was cut through the clay, lined with walls at the sides. The retaining walls at this time seem to have been made of sun-dried bricks. At the north end of the central passage a small stair shaft led to a wooden scene-building on top of the bank. At the sides parodoi were cut from the hillside to give access to the orchestra. This simple theater was used throughout the fourth century B.C., and it was rebuilt only near the end of the century.

A sunken orchestra necessitated certain constructions in the theater that would not have been required had the orchestra been on the natural ground level. Principal among these are the retaining walls along the scarp opposite the seats and probably also along the parodoi. Another was the need for direct access to the orchestra out of sight of the audience, which the central passage provided. Space inside the passage, however, was limited, and it could have had only one door leading to the orchestra. Unless the bank was cut away to provide room for a skene at orchestra level, some type of construction was desirable both in front of the bank and on top of it. This first seems to have taken the form of a narrow pro-skenion with a series of supports or possibly a solid front wall pierced by one or three doorways. Although productions involving a number of participants probably took place in the orchestra, it is possible that individual performers made use of the raised, albeit quite narrow, platform provided by the proskenion; and if dramatic works were presented at Isthmia, it would have made an admirable *theologeion*.[1] The fact that a narrow proskenion was built at orchestra level would almost certainly have required that a larger scene-building be built on top of the bank. These constructions, then, were related to the sunken orchestra, but they may have existed at the same time in other theaters that did not have this feature.[2]

Other theaters built on a rectilinear plan are known for the fifth and fourth centuries B.C.[3] Perhaps the closest parallels to Isthmia are the early theaters at Syracuse and Argos where the cavea was also cut from the side of a hill. Wherever the seating consisted of wooden benches, the auditorium would certainly have been arranged on straight lines. Stone foundations for seats, probably of wood, have in fact been recovered in the Theater of Dionysos at Athens dating from the end of the fifth century B.C. Other examples of straight seats are found at Rhamnous and Ikaria, where a simple line of stone proedria thrones comprised the entire permanent seating facility. At Tegea only two rows of the cavea have so far been uncovered—an original straight stone proedria bench and a row of thrones that was placed in front of the bench at a later time. The rows of straight seats at Morgantina lie high up the slope and may have belonged to one wing of a trapezoidal cavea. In none of these instances is there any evidence for a circular orchestra. On the contrary, the orchestra would have been the open area between the cavea and the skene, or its equivalent, delimited only by the drainage channel or curb where these were present. The drainage channel that follows the line of the auditorium at Tegea, and probably at Syracuse and at Isthmia, gave a boundary to the orchestra area that had no other apparent definition. The stone curb at Tegea, probably added with the thrones, is in a similar position. There are relatively few theaters,

1. Pseudo-Lucian records that tragedies or comedies were not customary at the Isthmian games until Nero demanded a performance of tragedy in which he could star on the occasion of his visit, probably in A.D. 66 (*Nero*, 9). The date of this information leaves the occurrence of such contests open to question with regard to the fourth century B.C., although there is no other evidence to the contrary. The first mention of a musical contest that would have taken place in the theater is not earlier than 310 B.C. (see below, p. 140).

2. The Theater of Dionysos at Athens as reconstructed in the time of Nikias (according to Dinsmoor, *AAG*, p. 210; *Studies*, I, 314 ff.) may well have had a long narrow wooden skene in front of wall H. There is a series of ten post holes in H, and it has been suggested by Dinsmoor, Fiechter, and others that more post holes were arranged in rows in front of the wall and that they were used in connection with a wooden scene-building. Webster defines this construction as a passage-like building about 2.26 m wide (*Bulletin of the John Rylands Library* 42 [1960]: 502–5). He compares it to the remains of the first skene in the theater at Corinth that consist of two rows of post holes about 4 m apart, which appear to have been used for a long, narrow wooden building (see Stillwell, *Theatre*, pp. 32–33). Arnott suggests that the holes were used for timbers to support a low stage, 1 m high and 4 m deep (*Scenic Conventions*, pp. 11–12). Both at Athens and Corinth the buildings are restored as the skene, but they are of the same long, narrow shape as the proskenion in the first theater at Isthmia and would have served much the same purpose.

3. See chap. 1, pp. 15–17, and nn. 13–19 for references relating to these theaters.

even among those with a fully developed curvilinear auditorium, in which a circular orchestra is marked off as a separate entity, and in all cases they are large and elaborate structures dating from the latter part of the fourth century B.C. or later; i.e., the theaters at Epidauros, Corinth, Argos, Oiniadai, and perhaps Ephesos.

From the evidence outlined above together with that examined in the theater at Isthmia, it may be concluded that the form of theaters early in date or of simple construction was not predetermined by a circular orchestra. Rather, it was the cavea, the largest element in terms of construction and expense, that fixed the shape of the orchestra.[4]

The Second and Third Greek Periods

The Isthmian theater was completely rebuilt near the end of the fourth century B.C., and the cavea was recut in the shape of an arched window, curved center with straight sides. The change to a curved seating arrangement here and elsewhere may well have resulted from the desire to provide a better view for a greater number of spectators and from the discovery of the superior acoustical properties of a curved form. At this time, then, the seat foundations were recut, and a paved walk that partially covered the abandoned drainage channels and manhole 1 was provided at the edge of the orchestra. The altar in the orchestra appears to have remained undisturbed. A new, deeper proskenion was built along the front of the clay bank at orchestra level, probably with wooden supports resting on a wooden sill. The mud-brick retaining wall for the bank was replaced in stone, as were the walls of the central passage. A stairway leading to the outside was built at the north end of the passage. On top of the bank the skene may also have been repaired or rebuilt. At either side of the parodoi gently sloping ramps led up to the top of the proskenion.

The wooden sill of the proskenion cannot have been very durable due to the moisture in the ground, and it was probably replaced by a stone sill before many years had passed. A restored plan of the theater at this time is given in Plate IV.

The new proskenion façade consisted of twelve rectangular wooden supports, and the intervals between them were closed by a series of panels that turned on pivots in the manner of swinging doors. These would have been easy to open for entrance into the orchestra through any one of the openings. The center opening was fitted with a double-leaf door. The panels may have been painted with appropriate designs to make a decorative façade, as has been suggested in the conjectural restoration of the proskenion (Pl. VII). It is altogether likely that individual performers, as the lyre-player in the drawing, would have used the top of the proskenion for

4. See chap. 1, p. 14, n. 12.

their performances, although the presence of the swinging panels in the proskenion at orchestra level suggests that some action also took place in the orchestra.

The first indication of an event that would certainly have taken place in the theater at Isthmia is the inscription recording the victories of Nikokles, son of Aristokles. Found at Athens, the marble statue base carries the record of his career as a κιθαρῳδός, which includes the words ΙΣΘΜΙΑ ΠΡΩΤΟΣ surrounded by a pine wreath.[5] This has generally been taken to mean that he won the contest for κιθαρῳδοί when it was first established as part of the Isthmian festival. The inscription was at first dated not later than 310 B.C. on the basis of the letter forms,[6] but a date in the 260s has been suggested by A. Körte on other grounds.[7]

Other references to contests that would have taken place in the theater are few indeed, and most of them are of Imperial date. They will be mentioned below in connection with the later periods of the theater.

It is important to note here that the proskenion in the Isthmian theater belongs to the fourth century B.C. and was an integral part of the building from the beginning. There has been much discussion concerning the question of when the proskenion was first introduced into the Greek theater. Although both Allen and Flickinger suggested one for the fifth century at Athens,[8] it is now generally affirmed that the first temporary, screenlike proskenion was created at Athens to meet the requirements of New Comedy (about 315 B.C.), which needed a "raised stage for clarity of vision, but shallow to give the effect of relief."[9] Pickard-Cambridge describes it as a "decorative screen (or curtains)" erected when required by the action.[10] This temporary screen is then considered to have been introduced into other existing theaters shortly thereafter.[11] Dinsmoor places the first proskenion planned as part of the original construction not earlier

5. *IG* 2/3, Part 2 (3), No. 3779.

6. U. Köhler, "Exegetisch-kritische Anmerkungen zu den Fragmenten des Antigonos von Karystos," *Rheinisches Museum* 39 (1884): 298 f.

7. Körte bases his argument primarily on the date for games at Alexandria called "Basilea," which are also mentioned in the inscription ("Zu attischen Dionysos-Festen," *Rheinisches Museum* 52 [1897]: 174 ff.). Schneider dates the inscription in either the fourth or third century B.C. (*RE* 9, Part 2 [1916]: 2252).

8. J. Allen, "The Greek Theater of the Fifth Century Before Christ," *University of California Publications in Classical Philology* 7 (1919): 110–16; R. Flickinger, *The Greek Theater and Its Drama* (4th ed.; Chicago: University of Chicago Press, 1936), pp. 68, 235 ff. See also Arnott, who proposed a low, deep stage for the fifth-century theaters at Athens, Corinth, Oropos, and Thorikos (*Scenic Conventions*, pp. 6 ff.). His argument is based primarily on evidence from the fifth-century plays and does not deal in detail with the location and construction of the scene-building.

9. Dinsmoor, *AAG*, p. 298.

10. Packard-Cambridge, *The Theatre of Dionysos*, p. 159. The evidence for other proskenia in the fourth century B.C. besides the one at Isthmia is presented above, chap. 2, p. 55, n. 42.

11. Dinsmoor, *AAG*, p. 299.

than the third century B.C. Although he remarks that a proskenion would have been necessary from the beginning in theaters with a sunken orchestra, especially those at Eretria and Corinth where there is no ground floor in the skene, he moves the date of their construction into the third century because of his assumption that no permanent proskenion could have existed earlier than that.[12] The very same assumption, however, led Fiechter to deny that a proskenion was included in the first rebuilding of the theater at Eretria because he believed that it was to be dated to the fourth century B.C.[13]

This is only a small indication of the importance attached to the date for the introduction of the proskenion and the effect it has had on the chronology of Greek theaters. Unfortunately, in no instance is the evidence furnished by the remains themselves sufficiently abundant or conclusive to settle the question. Nevertheless, the role of the proskenion as an integral part of the design in theaters with a sunken orchestra should be kept in mind. In these cases the proskenion was not merely a decorative feature added or removed at will, nor was it invented for the exhibition of New Comedy, but it was an important part of the scene-building. At Isthmia the date for the fully developed proskenion seems to fall in the late fourth century B.C., and it is to be hoped that more concrete evidence for the chronology of the other theaters with sunken orchestras will one day be forthcoming.

The First Roman Period

While the city of Corinth lay deserted for the century following its sack by Mummius in 146 B.C., it is not likely that the games at Isthmia prospered. Pausanius (ii 2.2) reports that they continued under the direction of Sikyon, probably at Sikyon. Even after Corinth was recolonized in 44 B.C., the Isthmian sanctuary had to wait for restoration and new buildings. It was not until the time of Nero that any major alterations were undertaken in the theater, and it may have been the prospect of his visit in A.D. 66 that gave added impetus to the project. Singing was Nero's special talent, and appropriate preparations for his imperial presence would have been particularly important in the theater.

The lower part of the auditorium was completely rebuilt and furnished with eight rows of stone seats. Above these a large addition was planned, although it never reached completion. At the foot of the lower seats a narrow gutter or a paved passage ran around the edge of the orchestra. The central drain in its present form began in the orchestra and ran northward along the axis of the theater. The scene-building was enlarged by the

12. Ibid., p. 300, n. 1.
13. Fiechter, *Ant. Th.* 8: 34–37.

addition of wings at either side that reached to the ends of the parodoi (Pl. I).

The center section of the skene also must have been rebuilt at this time, probably along the lines of its predecessor, at least in plan. Its outline is indicated by the position of the wings. The retaining walls for the center scarp, for the central passage, and for the north sides of the parodoi remained standing and received a new coat of plaster. The old proskenion would have disappeared, and it is not altogether clear what type of platform took its place. We can be sure, however, that it had approximately the same dimensions.

Earth was brought in to level the area to the northeast of the skene, and the first northeast building was built there. A north-south boundary wall divided the open space between the building and the cavea.

An inscription from Corinth records a list of victors in the Isthmian Caesarean games for A.D. 3. The contests for trumpeters, heralds, poets, encomiographers, flute-players, lyre-players, and those who sang to the lyre most naturally would have been held in a theater. Thus, perhaps the theater at Isthmia was provided with temporary new wooden furnishings, or the musical and literary contests were held in the theater at Corinth where the stone skene was in better condition.[14]

Later authors mention Nero's appearance at the Isthmian games and his victories in the musical contests that would have been particularly important to him. He carried off, undoubtedly to the sound of great applause, first prize in the harp and herald competitions; and probably later, at the time he initiated an attempt to cut through the isthmus, he sang a hymn to Amphitrite and Poseidon and a short song to Melicertes and Leucothea.[15]

Further light on the variety of competitions held in the theater is shed by an inscribed base built into the trans-Isthmian wall. The inscription records that Themison of Miletus won ninety-four victories at Isthmia, Nemea, and elsewhere, μόνον καὶ πρῶτον Εὐρειπίδην Σοφοκλέα καὶ Τειμόθεον ἑαυτῶ[ι] μελοποιήσαντα.[16]

This would appear to mean that he took works or parts of works from these authors and set them to music, and that he was the first and only person to develop and practice this art form. The inscription is assigned to the first half of the second century A.D.

14. B. Meritt, *Greek Inscriptions, 1896–1927*, Vol. 8, Pt. 1, of *Corinth: Results of the Excavations Conducted by the American School of Classical Studies at Athens* (Cambridge: Harvard University Press, 1931) 14–25, no. 14. The renovation of the buildings, which appears to have been carried out by L. Castricius Regulus when he restored the games to Isthmia in 6 B.C. or 2 B.C., left no trace in the theater. See Kent, *Inscriptions*, 70–73, no. 153.

15. Pseudo-Lucian, *Nero*, 3, records the songs, Philostratus the harp and herald contests, τὰ ἐς τὸν Τυανέα Ἀπολλώνιον, iv. 24.

16. Broneer, *Hesperia* 22 (1953): 192–93.

Victors in the Caesarea of A.D. 127 are listed on a stele recently found in Corinth. The Caesarea, a quadrennial festival, had a separate program but was held in conjunction with the Isthmian games and had the same *agonothetes*. The musical and literary contests are the same as those listed for A.D. 3 except that χ[οροκιθ]αρεῖς and χ[οραύλα]ς replace the flute-players and lyre-players. Added to the list are competitions for child comic actors, child singers to the lyre, comic poets, scene painters, comic actors, and tragic actors.[17]

The Second Roman Period

The theater reached its greatest expanse during the second half of the second century, perhaps during the reign of Marcus Aurelius or later. A restored plan of the theater at this time is given in Plate VIII.

The scheme of enlarging the cavea was taken up again, and concrete piers were laid in a semicircle on the periphery. This project, however, like the earlier one, was abandoned before it ever rose above the foundations. In the orchestra two tall Ionic columns provided an ornamental frame for the performers in front of the skene. A new proskenion with a solid front wall was erected on the old stone sill. Six statues or columns supported on piers beneath the proskenion floor may have decorated the front of the scene-building. The center section of the skene was rebuilt in rubble masonry, the foundations of which are still visible (Pl. I), and it appears to have retained the plan of the earlier buildings because the wings and central passage remained virtually unchanged. The central passage, how-ever, did receive a concrete vault, and the steps at the north end were re-constructed a little farther north where there would have been an entrance into the court behind the skene. The walls of the wings were reinforced with stone piers, and the south walls were moved back (northward) to rest on the new, heavy walls that supported the barrel vaults over the parodoi. The concrete vaults over the parodoi served to join the cavea to the scene-building, and *tribunalia* for distinguished spectators may have been built on top of them.

The area north of the skene was now included in the theater complex (Pl. VIII). A large open court was constructed with roads along three sides, and a stoa appears to have been planned for the fourth side but never com-pleted. West of the west road the slope of the hill was divided into two terraces by long retaining walls, and a small stairway connected them with the road. Along the eastern road the space was occupied by a storeroom at the south end next to the cavea and perhaps by a series of temporary

17. W. Biers and D. Geagan, "A New List of Victors in the Caesarea at Isthmia," *Hesperia* 39 (1970): 79 ff., ll. 16–56. See also D Geagan, "Notes on the Agonistic Institutions of Roman Corinth," *Greek, Roman, and Byzantine Studies* 9 (1968): 69 ff.

structures or booths erected at the time of the festivals between the store-room and the northeast building, which was rebuilt at this time.

A considerable amount of money was expended on the theater in this remodeling, but it was not transformed into a typical Roman theater, as was so often the case in Greek theaters extensively remodeled during the Imperial epoch; e.g., at Athens, Corinth, Argos, Sikyon, and Syracuse. Nor did the theater merely continue unaltered in its original Greek form as did the theaters at Epidauros and Eretria. At Isthmia an attempt was made to combine Greek and Roman forms in the same structure. The Greek element was represented mainly by the narrow, high proskenion, the deep scene-building, and the slanting orientation of the parodoi. No deep stage projected into the orchestra; there was no elaborate *scaenae frons*.[18] The purely Roman features include the barrel vaults over the parodoi and central passage and the court with its entrance roads, which made the theater into an architectural complex much favored by the Romans.

The nature of the contests held in the theater may be the reason why the Greek forms, especially the proskenion, were retained in the new construction of the Roman period. From the meager evidence available, it may be inferred that the contests in the theater remained substantially the same from the fourth century B.C. to the end of the third century A.D. when performances seem to have come to an end. The competitions were musical, literary, and then dramatic,[19] and the requirements for them would have been the same throughout. The proskenion made an ideal platform for the solo performances of poets, singers, and heralds, and classical Greek plays may also have been revived in the old manner in the orchestra. The theater thus retained its predominantly Greek form for some seven hundred years.

18. It should be borne in mind that only the foundations are preserved and that varied architectural effects would have been possible with the use of paint and plaster in conjunction with the columns or statues that may have been supported by the piers under the proskenion floor.

19. Schneider (*RE* 9, Part 2 [1916]: 2252) and J. Krause (*Die Pythien, Nemeen und Isthmien aus den Schriff—und Bildwerken des Altertums* [Leipzig: J. A. Barth, 1841], pp. 188 ff.), Meritt (*Inscriptions*, nos. 14, 15) and Biers and Geagan (*Hesperia* 39 [1970]: 79 ff.) give the basic evidence for the competitions. A new inscription commemorating the victories of a πυθαύλης of the second or third century A.D. will be published by Paul Clement.

Bibliography

Allen, H. "Excavations at Morgantina, 1967–1969, Preliminary Report X," *American Journal of Archaeology* 74 (1970): 359 ff.

Allen, J. "The Greek Theater of the Fifth Century Before Christ," University of California Publications in Classical Philology 7 (1919): 110 ff.

Anti, C. *Teatri Greci Arcaici.* Padua: Le Tre Venezie, 1947.

Arias, P. *Il Teatro greco fuori di Atene.* Florence: G. S. Sansoni, 1934.

Arnott, P. *Greek Scenic Conventions of the Fifth Century B.C.* Oxford: Clarendon Press, 1962.

Bernabo Brea, L. "Studi sul teatro greco di Siracusa," *Palladio* 17 (1967), 97 ff.

de Bernardi Ferrero, D. *Teatri Classici in Asia Minore: 2, Città di Pisidia, Licia e Caria, Studi di Architettura Antica.* Rome: L'Erma di Bretschneider, 1969.

Bethe, E. "Der Spielplatz des Aischylos," *Hermes* 59 (1924): 108 ff.

Bieber, M. *The History of the Greek and Roman Theater.* 2d ed., revised. Princeton: Princeton University Press, 1961.

Biers, W. "Excavations at Phlius, 1970," *Hesperia* 40 (1971): 424 ff.

Biers, W., and Geagan, D. "A New List of Victors in the Caesarea at Isthmia," *Hesperia* 39 (1970): 79 ff.

Broneer, O. "The Apostle Paul and the Isthmian Games," *The Biblical Archaeologist* 25 (1962): 2 ff.

———. "Excavations at Isthmia, 1954," *Hesperia* 24 (1955): 122 ff.

———. "Excavations at Isthmia, 1955–1956," *Hesperia* 27 (1958): 1 ff.

———. "Excavations at Isthmia, Fourth Campaign, 1957–1959," *Hesperia* 38 (1959): 298 ff.

———. "Excavations at Isthmia, 1959–1961," *Hesperia* 31 (1962): 1 ff.

———. "Isthmia: Campaign of 1959," *Archaeology* 13 (1960): 105 ff.

———. "Isthmia Excavations, 1952," *Hesperia* 22 (1953): 182 ff.

———. *Isthmia I: Temple of Poseidon.* Princeton: The American School of Classical Studies at Athens, 1971.

———. "Isthmiaca," *Klio* 39 (1961): 249 ff.

———. "The Isthmian Victory Crown," *American Journal of Archaeology* 66 (1962): 259 ff.

———. *The Odeum,* Vol. 10 of *Corinth: Results of the Excavations Conducted by the American School of Classical Studies at Athens.* Cambridge, Mass.: Harvard University Press, 1932.

———. "The ΟΧΕΤΟΣ in the Greek Theater," in *Classical Studies Presented to Edward Capps,* pp. 29 ff. Princeton: Princeton University Press, 1936.

———. *The South Stoa and Its Roman Successors,* Vol 1, Part IV, of *Corinth: Results of the Excavations Conducted by the American School of Classical Studies at Athens.* Princeton: The American School of Classical Studies at Athens, 1954.

————. "The Temple of Poseidon at Isthmia," *Χαριστήριον εἰς Ἀναστάσιον Κ. Ὀρλάνδον*, 3:61 ff. 4 vols. Athens: Ἀρχαιολογικὴ Ἑταιρεία, 1965–68.

————. *Terracotta Lamps.* Vol. 4, Part II, of *Corinth: Results of the Excavations Conducted by the American School of Classical Studies at Athens.* Cambridge, Mass.: Harvard University Press, 1930.

Brownson, C., and Young, C. "Further Excavations in the Theater at Sicyon, 1891," *Papers of the American School of Classical Studies in Athens* 6 (1890–97): 10 ff.

Buck, C. "Discoveries in the Attic Deme of Ikaria, 1888: Architectural Remains," *American Journal of Archaeology* 5 (1889): 165 ff.

Bulle, H. *Untersuchungen an griechischen Theatern.* Vol. 33 of the *Abhandlungen der bayerischen Akademie der Wissenschaften, Philologische-historische Klasse.* Munich: R. Oldenbourg, 1928.

Bursian, C. *Geographie von Griechenland.* 2 vols. Leipzig: Teubner, 1868–72.

Cailler, P., and Cailler, D. *Les Théâtres Gréco-Romains de Gréce.* Volume 1 of *Style.* 1966.

Calza, G., and Becatti, G. *Ostia.* Rome: Istituto Poligrafico dello Stato, 1955.

Canac, F. *L'Acoustique des Théâtres Antiques, ses Enseignements.* Paris Editions du Centre National de la Recherche Scientifique, 1967.

Caputo, G. "Note sugli edifici teatrali della Cirenaica," in *Anthemon*, pp. 281 ff. Florence: G. C. Sansoni, 1955.

Clement, P. "Isthmia," *Ἀρχαιολογικὸν Δελτίον* 23 (1968): 137 ff.

————. "Isthmia," *Ἀρχαιολογικὸν Δελτίον* 24 (1969): 116 ff.

Chamonard, S. "Théâtre de Delos," *Bulletin de Correspondance Hellénique* 20 (1896): 256 ff.

Corbett, P. "Attic Pottery of the Later Fifth Century from the Athenian Agora," *Hesperia* 18 (1949): 298 ff.

Couve, L. "Isthmia," *Dictionnaire des Antiquités Grecques et Romaines* 3, Part 1. Edited by C. Daremberg and E. Saglio, pp. 588 ff. 1899.

Curtius, E. *Peloponnesos.* 2 vols. Gotha: Justus Perthes, 1851–52.

Dakari, S. "Τὸ Ἱερὸν τῆς Δωδώνης," *Ἀρχαιολογικὸν Δελτίον* 16 (1960): 4 ff.

Daux, G. "Chronique des Fouilles et Découvertes Archéologiques en Grèce en 1958," *Bulletin de Correspondance Hellénique* 83 (1959): 568 ff.

————. "Chronique des Fouilles et Découvertes archéologiques en Grèce en 1963," *Bulletin de Correspondance Hellénique* 88 (1964): 681 ff.

Daux, G., and Laumonier, A. "Fouilles de Thasos, 1921–22," *Bulletin de Correspondance Hellénique* 47 (1923): 315 ff.

Dilke, O. "Details and Chronology of Greek Theatre Caveas," *Annual of the British School at Athens* 45 (1950): 21 ff.

———. "The Greek Theatre Cavea," *Annual of the British School at Athens* 43 (1948): 125 ff.

Dinsmoor, W. The Architecture of Ancient Greece. 3d ed., revised. London: B. T. Batsford, 1950.

———. "The Athenian Theater of the Fifth Century," in *Studies Presented to David M. Robinson*, 1:309 ff. 2 vols. Saint Louis: Washington University Press, 1951.

Dörpfeld, W. "Die Arbeiten zu Pergamon 1904–1905: Das griechische Theater der Akropolis," *Mitteilungen des kaiserlich deutschen archäologischen Instituts: Athenische Abteilung* 32 (1907): 215 ff.

———. "Das Theater von Priene und die griechische Bühne," *Mitteilungen des deutschen archäologischen Instituts: Athenische Abteilung* 49 (1924): 50 ff.

———. *Troja und Ilion*. Athens: Beck and Barth, 1902.

Dörpfeld, W., and Reisch, E. *Das Griechische Theater*. Athens: Barth and von Hirst, 1896.

Edwards, K. *Coins*. Volume 6 of *Corinth: Results of the Excavations Conducted by the American School of Classical Studies in Athens*. Cambridge, Mass.: Harvard University Press, 1933.

Else, G. *The Origin and Early Form of Greek Tragedy*. Cambridge, Mass.: Harvard University Press, 1965.

Fiechter, E. *Antike griechische Theaterbauten*. Volume 1: *Das Theater in Oropos*. Volume 2: *Die Theatern von Oiniadai und Neu-Pleuron*. Volume 3: *Das Theater in Sikyon*. Volume 4: *Das Theater in Megalopolis*. Volume 5: *Das Dionysos-Theater in Athen: Die Ruine*. Volume 6: *Das Dionysos-Theater in Athen: Die übrigen baulichen Reste und die Geschichte Baues*. Volume 8: *Das Theater in Eretria*. Volume 9: *Das Dionysos Theater in Athen: Nachträge, Das Theater in Piraieus, Das Theater auf Thera*. Stuttgart: W. Kohlhammer, 1930–50.

———. *Die Baugeschichtliche Entwicklung des Antikens Theaters*. Munich: O. Beck, 1914.

Flickinger, R. *The Greek Theater and Its Drama*. 4th ed. Chicago: University of Chicago Press, 1936.

———. "The Theater of Aeschylus," *Transactions and Proceedings of the American Philological Association* 61 (1930): 80 ff.

Formigé, J. *Remarques Diverses sur les Théâtres Romains*. Paris: C. Klincksieck, 1914.

Fougerès, G. *Maintineé et l'Arcadie Orientale*. Paris: A. Fontemoing, 1898.

Fox, E. "The Duoviri of Corinth," *Journal International d'Archéologie Numismatique* 2 (1899): 89 ff.

Fuchs, W., and Tusa, A. "Archäologische Forschungen und Funde in Sizilien von 1955 bis 1964," *Archäologische Anzeiger* 4 (1964): 657 ff.

Geagan, D. "Notes on the Agonistic Institutions of Roman Corinth," *Greek, Roman, and Byzantine Studies* 9 (1968): 69 ff.

von Gerkan, A. *Das Theater von Priene*. Munich-Berlin: F. Schmidt, 1921.

———. "Zu den Theatern von Segesta und Tyndaris," in *Festschrift Andreas Rumpf*, pp. 82 ff. Krefeld: Scherpe, 1952.

von Gerkan, A., and Müller-Wiener, W. *Das Theater von Epidauros*. Stuttgart: W. Kohlhammer, 1961.

Ginouvès, R. "Chronique des Fouilles en 1955: Argos," *Bulletin de Correspondance Hellénique* 80 (1956): 361 ff.

———. "Chronique des Fouilles en 1956: Argos," *Bulletin de Correspondance Hellénique* 81 (1957): 637 ff.

———. "Chronique des Fouilles en 1958: Argos," *Bulletin de Correspondance Hellénique* 83 (1959): 754 ff.

Hackens, T. "Thorikos 1963: Le Théâtre," *L'Antiquité Classique* 34 (1965): 39 ff.

———. "Le Théâtre," *Thorikos 1965* 3 (1967): 75 ff.

Hammond, M. "The Tribunician Day During the Early Empire," *Memoirs of the American Academy at Rome* 15 (1938): 23 ff.

Hill, I., and King, L. *Decorated Architectural Terracottas*. Volume 4, Part I, of *Corinth: Results of Excavations Conducted by the American School of Classical Studies at Athens*. Cambridge, Mass.: Harvard University Press, 1929.

Jacopi, G. "Il Tempio e il teatro di Apollo Eretimio," *Clara Rhodos* 2 (1932): 79 ff.

Jeffery, L. *The Local Scripts of Archaic Greece*. Oxford: Clarendon Press, 1961.

Jenkins, F., and Megaw, H. "Researches at Isthmia," *Annual of the British School at Athens* 32 (1931–1932): 68 ff.

Judeich, W. *Topographie von Athen*, Vol. 2, Part II, Section 3, of *Handbuch der Altertumswissenschaft*, edited by W. Otto. Munich: C. H. Beck, 1931.

Kardara, C. "Dyeing and Weaving Works at the Isthmia," *American Journal of Archaeology* 65 (1961): 261 ff.

Kent, J. *The Inscriptions, 1926–1950*. Vol. 8, Part III, of *Corinth: The Results of the Excavations Conducted by the American School of Classical Studies at Athens*. Princeton: American School of Classical Studies at Athens, 1966.

Köhler, U. "Exegetisch-kritische Anmerkungen zu den Fragmenten des Antigonos von Karystos," *Rheinisches Museum* 39 (1884): 293 ff.

Körte, A. "Zu attischen Dionysos-Festen," *Rheinisches Museum* 52 (1897): 168 ff.

Krause, J. *Die Pythien, Nemeen und Isthmien aus den Schrift-Bildwerken des Altertums*. Leipzig: J. A. Barth, 1841.

Leon V., and St. Karwiese. "Griechenland: Ellis," *Osterreichisches archäologisches Instituts, Grabungen 1965*. Baden bei Wien: Rudolf Rohrer, 1966. Pp. 13 ff.

Levi, M. *Nereone e i suoi tempi*. Milan: Istituto editoriale Cisalpino, 1949.

Libertini, G. "Scavi di Lemnos," *Annuario della Regia Scuola Archeologica di Atene, N. S.* 1–2 (1939–40): 221 ff.

Pseudo-Lucian. *Nero, sive de fossione Isthmi*. Translated by M. Macleod. Vol. 8 of *Lucian* in the Loeb Classical Library. Cambridge, Mass.: Harvard University Press, 1967.

Lugli, G. *La Tecnia edilizia romana*. 2 vols. Rome: Giovanni Bardi, 1957.

MacDowall, D. "Countermarks of Early Imperial Corinth," *Numismatic Chronicle*. 7th series, vol. 2 (1962): 113 ff.

Martin, R. "Matériaux et Techniques." Part 1 of *Manuel d' Architecture Grecque*. Paris: A. and J. Picard, 1965.

Mattingly, H. *Coins of the Roman Empire in the British Museum*. 6 vols. Oxford: The University Press, 1940.

Meritt, B. *Greek Inscriptions, 1896–1927*, Vol. 8, Part I, of *Corinth: Results of the Excavations Conducted by the American School of Classical Studies at Athens*. Cambridge: Harvard University Press, 1931.

Meritt, L. "The Geographical Distribution of Greek and Roman Ionic Bases," *Hesperia* 38 (1969): 186 ff.

Momigliano, A. "Nero," in *The Cambridge Ancient History* 10: 702 ff. 12 vols. Cambridge: The University Press, 1934.

Monceaux, P. "Fouilles et Recherches Archéologiques au Sanctuaire des Jeux Isthmiques," *Gazette Archéologique* 10 (1885): 208 ff.

Neppi Modona, A. *Gli Edifici teatrali greci e romani*. Florence: Leo Olschki, 1961.

Pease, M. "A Well of the Late Fifth Century at Corinth," *Hesperia* 6 (1937): 257 ff.

Picard, C. "Fouilles de Thasos, (1914 et 1920)," *Bulletin de Correspondance Hellénique* 45 (1921): 86 ff.

Pickard-Cambridge, A. *The Dramatic Festivals of Athens*. Rev. by J. Gould and D. Lewis. Oxford: Clarendon Press, 2d ed., 1968.

———. *The Theatre of Dionysos in Athens*. Oxford: Clarendon Press, 1946.

Pollux, *Onomasticon*. Ed. by E. Bethe. Leipzig: Teubner, 1900.

Pouilloux, J. *La Fortresse de Rhamnonte*. Paris: E. de Boccard, 1954.

Powell, B. "Oeniadae: The Theatre," *American Journal of Archaeology* 8 (1904): 174 ff.

Rizzo, G. *Il Teatro Greco di Siracusa*. Milan: Bestetti and Tumminelli, 1923.

Robinson, D. *Excavations at Olynthus*. Volume 5: *Mosaics, Vases and Lamps of Olynthus*. Volume 13: *Vases Found in 1934 and 1938*. 14 vols. Baltimore: Johns Hopkins Press, 1933, 1950.

Robinson, H. *Pottery of the Roman Period—Chronology*. Volume 5 of *The Athenian Agora, Results of Excavations Conducted by the American School of Classical Studies*. Princeton: The American School of Classical Studies at Athens, 1959.

Roux, G. "Chronique des Fouilles en 1953: Argos," *Bulletin de Correspondance Hellénique* 78 (1954): 158 ff.

———. "Chronique des Fouilles et Découvertes Archéologiques en Grèce en 1955: Seconde Partie. Argos: Le Théâtre," *Bulletin de Correspondance Hellénique* 80 (1956): 376 ff.

———. *Pausanius en Corinthie* (Book 2, 1 à 15), Paris: Société d' Edition Les Belles Lettres, 1958.

Salviat, F. "Le Bâtiment de Scène du Théâtre de Thasos," *Bulletin de Correspondance Hellénique* 84 (1960): 300 ff.

Schefold, K. "Die Grabungen in Eretria im Herbst 1964 und 1965: Das Theater," *Antike Kunst* 9 (1966): 110 ff.

Schneider, K. "Isthmia," *Pauly's Realencyclopädie der klassischen Altertumswissenschaft*. Edited by K. Ziegler. 2d series, 9, Part 2 (1916): 2248 ff.

Scranton, R. *Monuments in the Lower Agora and North of the Archaic Temple*. Vol. 1, Part III, of *Corinth: Results of the Excavations Conducted by the American School of Classical Studies at Athens*. Princeton: The American School of Classical Studies at Athens, 1951.

Shear, T. "Excavations in the Theatre District and Tombs of Corinth in 1929," *American Journal of Archaeology* 33 (1929): 515 ff.

Smith, E. "Prehistoric Pottery from the Isthmia," *Hesperia* 24 (1955): 142 ff.

Stillwell, R. *The Theatre*. Vol. 2 of *Corinth: Results of the Excavations Conducted by the American School of Classical Studies at Athens*. Princeton: The American School of Classical Studies at Athens, 1952.

Sydenham, E. *The Coinage of Nero*. London: Spink and Son, Ltd., 1920.

Talbot-Rice, D. (ed.). *The Great Palace of the Byzantine Emperors*. Edinburgh: The University Press, 1958.

Thompson, H. "Two Centuries of Hellenistic Pottery," *Hesperia* 3 (1934): 311 ff.

Vallois, R. *Architecture hellénique et hellénistique a Délos.* 2 vols. Paris: E. de Boccard, 1944.

————. "Le Théâtre de Tégée," *Bulletin de Correspondance Hellénique* 50 (1926): 135 ff.

Vitruvius, *De Architectura.* Translated with notes by S. Ferri. Rome: Palombi, 1960.

Vogliano, A., and Cumont, F. "La grande Iscrizione Bacchica del Metropolitan Museum," *American Journal of Archaeology* 37 (1933): 215 ff.

Vogt, J. *Die alexandrinischen Münzen.* Stuttgart: W. Kohlhammer, 1924.

Walter, O. "Vorläüfiger Bericht über die Grabungen in Elis, 1914," *Jahreshefte des österreichischen archäologischen Instituts in Wein* 18 (1915): 61 ff.

Webster, T. B. L. *Greek Theatre Production.* London: Methuen, 1956.

————. "South Italian Vases and Attic Drama," *Classical Quarterly* 42 (1948): 18 ff.

————. "Staging and Scenery in the Ancient Greek Theatre," *Bulletin of the John Rylands Library* 42 (1960): 493 ff.

Wieseler, F. *Theatergebäude und Denkmäler des Bühnenwesens bei den Griechen und Römern.* Göttingen: Vandenhœck und Ruprecht, 1851.

Index